The Power
of an
Untamed Mindset

The Power
of an
Untamed Mindset

A Story of Resilience

Kodjo Adabra

gatekeeper press™

Tampa, Florida

The Power of an Untamed Mindset: A Story of Resilience

Published by Gatekeeper Press
7853 Gunn Hwy, Suite 209
Tampa, FL 33626
www.GatekeeperPress.com

The cover design, interior formatting, typesetting, and editorial work for this book are entirely the product of the author. Gatekeeper Press did not participate in and is not responsible for any aspect of these elements.

Library of Congress Control Number: 2022951242

ISBN (paperback): 9781662934926
eISBN: 9781662934933

To my father, Kossi-Agbalenyo, and my mother, Adjoa-Sedenou, for their brilliant idea of bringing me into this world.

Contents

Preface

July 2022

Since the earliest years of my childhood, I have always been grateful for the art of the written word. Perhaps I was grateful for it back then because the written word made it easy for me to assimilate knowledge, comprehend scholarly thoughts, and be a high academic achiever. Today, however, I'm grateful for the art of the written word because I can use it to tell my story in my own words with my voice. My story crisscrosses time, oceans, and distance. It is one of true inspiration and grace. My story has shaped me into a person valiantly unafraid to mute my voice—a person who holds pieces of my story like diamonds in the sunlight. And when I made up my mind that I was going to tell it, I decided I would hold nothing back. Not my fears, pain, wins, tragedies, losses, and joys. After all, that's what a memoir is all about, isn't it? Sitting down to write about your story in your own words, describing to others how the tapestries of your existence have molded you into the man or woman you have become?

So here I am, seated in my study on a beautiful and bright day with all the opulence that summer brings, a day that gives away nothing of what today's world has truly become. There's a lot I hope you'd take away from my story of course. What

I'm hoping to actively achieve the most with readers are union, trust, and hopefully, in the end, new and refreshing insights. Union and trust would ensure that you will be ready to walk in my shoes toward a deeper understanding of other cultures, ideologies, and experiences that may or may not be directly antithetical to yours.

I would be honest when I say I had conflicted thoughts and feelings about writing a memoir. After all, in today's time and age, a book is competing with everything that's not a book—TikTok videos, Instagram videos, YouTube videos, reality shows on television, etc. The attention of the average person is being pulled into so many directions that if you do not consciously make an effort to filter the kind of content you want to consume, all kinds of things will find their way toward you.

Thankfully, I had those who encouraged me along the way, those who rooted for me and told me indirectly that the power of my voice is not something I must lose despite the distraction from the digitized world. I will forever be grateful to those acquaintances and friends who have found my life story inspiring and empowering. This book is partly based upon the strength of their convictions. They have taught me that a story is something to be proud of. A story is something to own, and a truly human story is something that many in this world will either learn from or relate to. However, my true motivations for this book do not just stem from having a story of my own. They also stem from my worldviews on spirituality and my unique existential views about life and religion. It has always been quite ironic to me that those who are not active believers of any faith, when running for public office or have intentions, transform into falsely religious versions of themselves. It's like digging deep to find a caricature that fits their aspirations because they want to be seen as "good." Of course, good is relative, but I've always believed that *good* is a weighty word. It matters that it should be accessed from the content of a person's character and not just their religious affiliations.

Lastly, I guess it can easily be said that my unorthodox views on death and destiny complete my three-dimensional motivations for this book. I lost a close friend dear to my heart two years ago, and after his death, I was determined to stop postponing the writing of this book. I believe that death plays an elusive hide-and-seek game with us as humans, and quite frankly, I am not good at that game. My fear of death is nonexistent. It is an imminent, inevitable, and unpreventable natural cause that must take place. Therefore I have never understood how fear could sit with this understanding. Life, over the years, has been given distinctive conceptualizations by distinctive people. My conceptualization is a bridge. The commencement of that bridge is our birth, while the end is death. The length in between is our journey through life, which varies for everyone. I am content with whatever length my bridge is, but I am hopeful that my memoir will put me a step ahead of the hide-and-seek game with death.

As you can tell, I have a lot to say. Compiling a lifetime of memories, thought processes, trajectories, and undiluted experiences into seven chapters was not easy, but it was a necessary imperative. I hope that the weight of my story, convictions, and experiences resounds through distance and time, touching lives and touching people who will stay connected to this story for years to come. This is my hope. This is perhaps my biggest motivation. So relax, preferably with some popcorn and Coke or juice, and let me take you on a ride from the beauty of my homeland in Togo to the snow-strewn streets of America. It is a ride that I hope will not be easily erasable.

CHAPTER 1

Childhood and Immigration

The night of January 7, 1974, was a cold Monday night. I can't tell if there was anything or anyone particularly memorable about it. Still, precisely at five past nine, I sauntered into this world from my mother's womb as a screaming infant into the small but independent nation of Togo.

At the time of my birth, Togo, like most other African nations, had wrestled itself free from decades of prohibitive colonialism from the French, who still had the nation steeped fully in neocolonialist cultures. Back then, because of the dominant Christian culture in the southern region of Togo, most of us from that region were given three names: a traditional African name, a family name, and a French name that matched the name of the French saint on the calendar. The saint's name for January 7 is Raymond, and my family name is Adabra. In my tribe, the Ewe of Southern Togo, boys and girls are named primarily from the day of the week they came into the world, so automatically, I was named Kodjo, which means "Monday-born," being a male child. I was born Raymond Kodjo Adabra into the Adabra family as the third child out of six on the night of January 7, 1974.

I was born in the western part of Lome, the capital city, in a deeply ingrained cultural neighborhood called Kodjoviakope. It's still a notable neighborhood in Lome to date, with landmarks such as the Peace Corps Office, the Lycee Français School for French nationals, and the American International School.

One undeniably true thing about Kodjoviakope is how educationally conscious the neighborhood is. It still consists of a public high school and several public and private middle and elementary schools. At the time of my birth, my parents had built a house for themselves—a four-bedroom villa with a terrace and a garage, painted all white with tints of gray on the pillars. The house also had a spare two-bedroom apartment and three rooms that served as guest rooms. I loved our house growing up. It was also where I grew up with my five siblings and my cousins, who lived just across the road. Like most people, the details about my earliest years are splotchy at best. I'd always remember, though, that amid my parents, siblings, cousins who lived across the road, and community, I was loved loud and clear. The thriving bond of familial love was never truly absent.

I was disciplined loud and clear too. In my formative years, I quickly learned that, like most African communities, Kodjoviakope believed (and still believes) that it takes a community to raise a child. Since this ideological construct is ostensibly absent in the Western world, I'd explain a bit.

Simply put, every adult has the right to correct or discipline a wayward child or one showing telltale signs of towing the wrong path. Back then, in Lome, you didn't even need to tow a wrong path before being disciplined. So floggings characterized my early years a lot. It was not because I played truant or because I was disobedient; it was simply the natural order of things in our culture. If you didn't meet up with the standards of what was viewed as right, you were flogged and flogged until you met up with them. Those who grew up in my time in my homeland, or in any other part of the African soil, can fully attest to how analogous this is.

Today it amuses me quite a bit to see how floggings are vehemently avoided in the Western world. Perhaps if those floggings executed through the use of long, thin canes were to take place today in the United States, many students would seek solace in mental counseling while propounding theories of self-expression and self-determination. I can confidently state that floggings didn't traumatize me or anyone else I grew up with. But of course, the beatings weren't pleasant; they were hurtful, scary, and intimidating. The intensity that accompanied them made us kids scramble to do the right thing until doing the right things started to flow naturally within our veins. But no one got traumatized to a point where their mental health got bludgeoned until it plunged deeply into an abyss and they had to struggle to salvage it.

I once read somewhere about studies showing that physical punishment can greatly impede cognitive advancement and growth in life. In the case of my life and that of my peers, I didn't witness any damaging negative impact that came from all the physical discipline we were subjected to. I daresay it straightened us up and partially became a torchbearer to our varying life successes. Additionally, it cultivated an impressive spirit of resilience and instilled in us the strength and bravery to handle the tough curveballs of life. I can also say that physical discipline taught me about the art of striving in a Western environment and the appreciation of freedom.

Nevertheless, I sometimes envy the youth in the West and how they are fortunate enough to be shielded from physical discipline. Such protection is quite advantageous. It aids in faster growth as well as an easier learning process. If I seem to be talking too much about it, it's because it was almost sacrosanct. It was a given, and as kids, we accepted it as a given. Back then, physical discipline was an unwavering terror. Today it does nothing but bring a nostalgic smile to my face. It is, however, not a practice that I recommend or condone these days. I do not resent the adults in my life for it. After all, it was their way of training the child in a way that they should go. And at that point in my life, I was in no position to escape or avoid it, which made it easier to accept.

Lome was very beautiful to me while I was growing up. My formative years were in the '70s—when the Cold War raged within the first world, Southern Africa was locked in a battle with the brutal apartheid regime, and Africa was just coming into her own as a continent free from the shackles of colonialism as her leaders scrambled to solve internal developmental issues using Western strategies.

None of this registered with me as a kid. My world was two-dimensional, characterized only by family and school. Schooling was embedded in my life from an early age. I would walk to school every morning without any inherent fears about external dangers because those were simpler times, with fewer fears. The educational structure and its routine were something that I learned to adapt quickly to. My classes ran from seven up until noon, when we would be allowed to go for a break. I'd quickly walk home for lunch and then come back to school for my afternoon classes, which ran from three to five. Walking was fully steeped in my life, just as flogging was. School buses, cars, and school transportation were nonexistent.

Our teachers wasted no time disciplining us when it seemed as though we failed our assignments or classwork. I was fairly exempted from that because I was above average in school. My grades stood head, neck, and shoulders tall. My brain, bright as it was, shone with an incandescence that couldn't be diminished. Even as a child, I always enjoyed the thrill of accomplishments thrumming through my blood. I worked hard at my academics, and as my grades glittered at the end of the school year, I relished my small treats and victories. My grades distinguished me in the classroom, and I'll always remember them as my first taste of true success because I usually put in enormous effort to achieve them. Assignments, classwork, homework, and exams were always a breeze for me.

While I stood tall in academics, I was short in height, and as a result, I became short in self-esteem too. Now that I reflect upon it, I'm not surprised I felt that way, especially living in a world that approves of tallness in men. It is universally viewed as some form of masculine trait when a man is tall. Women are always more in love with tall men, and it has always been easy for a congenital trait like height to breed confidence because of that approval. Unconsciously, this mindset was inculcated and espoused in me as a child, and as such, I detested my height, which wasn't even up to five feet six. I blamed heredity for this, though, especially my dad. Before heading into the intricacies of the heredity issues that I struggled with, I'll tell you briefly about my folks.

I admired my parents a great deal. Growing up, my family was my everything. My parents, siblings, and cousins dominated a large dimension of it. I learned from them, played with them, ate with them, and fought with them. But my parents were by far the biggest influences in my childhood. My father, the patriarch of the Adabra family, was a man from another generation with a different perspective, life journey, belief, and ideological conviction. A man who had to reinvent himself in another time and place to ascend to bigger heights in life. He was a traditional man in every sense of the word. He prioritized education a great deal, and to date, I still hold immense gratitude in my heart toward him for his heavy investments in my education and my life as a whole.

Dad did everything he could to consistently ensure that our heads floated above water every time. We were never sunk in the seas of neglect, hunger, extreme poverty, or a lack of education, as opposed to most of the other inner-city kids who grew up without father figures in their lives. Watching those kids, I saw that it was evident that certain anomalies would crop up in their lives later on. I didn't stick around long enough to find out, though. I consider Dad the one who assiduously balanced our family firmly on his strong shoulders.

Mom, on the other hand, was the soul and heart. The one who bred existential warmth and molded our family with her hands. She took our well-being and overall growth very seriously and was mostly in charge of our home training. Dad challenged and stimulated us intellectually and always made sure we had food to eat and clothes on our backs; however, work took him away from us a great deal. So most times, we shared anecdotes and daily stories with our mother. She taught us most of the traditional songs, prepared us sumptuous meals, and took religion seriously. She didn't hesitate, too, to spank us whenever the need arose. If we were disrespectful, got physical with another child, or slacked in our chores and responsibilities, Mom was always there to straighten us up, preferably with a flogging. We didn't resent or hate her for this because, as I said earlier, floggings were fully embedded in our lives.

My mother didn't have a college education, but she understood the importance of education and prioritized it deeply, just as much as my dad. She made sure we understood its importance and its impact through her prioritization. In my dad's absence, she'd ensure schoolwork preceded everything else. One unforgettable memory I have of her is her asking my older siblings for their diplomas to keep them safe. And yeah, she did keep those papers safe. She might not have understood the words scrawled on them, but she understood the weight of their importance.

Perhaps the Christmas holidays are the brightest memories of my mother that remain undiminished even after all these years. Growing up, Christmas was the most celebrated and cherished holiday season. You can be sure that during the Christmas holidays, you'd eat your favorite meals, watch your favorite movies, and see those extended family members you hadn't seen or heard from in a while. Christmas was the season to look forward to, and it was treated specially in my household.

My siblings and I looked forward to it mainly because the promise of new clothing excited us. The six of us would happily tag along with our mother to the local tailor and get our measurements done, and shortly before Christmas Day, we'd have our handmade outfits uniquely tailored and designed for our body types, all cut from the same fabric. The practice was the norm until we got to middle school and it started to look quite comical. It was as though we were members of the same band or something. Of course, by the time we got to high school, we'd gotten too old to be getting the same fabric designs for Christmas, and thankfully, it stopped. But those years illustrated my mother's character and love for her children.

I didn't get to be buddies with Dad until I had grown up and gone to college because, as I mentioned, he was constantly away doing his best to provide for and support the family. Yet even in his absence, Dad was an inspiration to me in particular. I was intrigued by the significant level of authority he effortlessly commanded.

Dad was an executive administrator in public medicine, and he was highly respected by his peers and those he supervised. It was one of the first pivotal lessons I learned in life: To commandeer respect, size is of little importance; intelligence, on the other hand, has to be preeminent. Dad was a sound intellectual who had attended the University of Paris and received a doctor of law degree and a hospital management certificate from the Bordeaux International School in France. Armed with his powerful certifications from France, he returned to Togo and easily snagged a position as the assistant director of the University Hospital Center. Dad also worked as an administrator with the Red Cross Society in Togo, and afterward, he became a vice secretary in the nation's health cabinet, a position he held until he retired. Overall, he spent twenty-eight years of his life in public service.

While Dad's career was inspiring, I was more inspired by those around him who respected and looked up to him, irrespective of his short stature. Stature notwithstanding, Dad exhibited strong leadership skills and values both in his career and within the home. Of course, we gave him the title of the man of the house in our close-knit nuclear family. Within our extended family, he took his roles seriously as well. Our extended family members were never too far away and never too busy to show up for a visit. Phones were not so rampant in those days, so calling before coming to the house of a family or friend was a foreign concept. Families were tight and close-knit, and the whole in-house and in-your-face interactions pervaded our lives a lot. Dad was actively involved with his parents, siblings, cousins, and several distant relatives. So it was only natural that they became a part of our lives.

Dad felt a responsibility toward all of them because they existed in a consistent state of lack and want. Many of them weren't highly skilled enough to get well-paying jobs, nor were they highly educated. They lived on paltry sums of money, and as such, Dad took responsibility for their finances. Most of the time, he'd come through when some form of financial hardship engulfed them. He did his best to always soften whatever lack or want that they felt. Often I reflect on how my father had managed to carry his financial load without complaints. My mom was a full-time housewife, dedicated mostly to the home front. Unlike what is prevalent in today's world, where both couples financially manage a home, my dad was left all alone with the role of financial provider. He paid our fees, clothed us, and put a roof over our heads. Then he would take care of the endless needs of our extended family members, who visited all year long. Sometimes many visited not for financial help but simply to check up on him and his well-being. Even then, they would expect him to foot the transportation bills, and he would do so.

I never heard my father grumble or complain once about how burdensome or cumbersome it was for him to be financially responsible for all of us. Of course, as a kid and a teen, I was more concerned with other things, like basketball and high school, than my dad's feelings about our finances. Yet even then, and even now as an adult, my gratitude toward him has never in any way dissolved, and it never will. I'll always believe that his extreme sense of responsibility emanated from his love for family and the total acceptance that he was the central, cohesive source of stability we all had even though he didn't qualify as rich or upper middle class. To date, this is prevalent among most men in the African continent and even within the black community as a whole. Most of all, Dad unconsciously taught me that respect is earned. And he earned his respect through his indomitable leadership at home with family and in his work in public service.

The realization that my height didn't matter in the grand scheme of things recalibrated my mind and pushed me to work harder at my grades. Good grades made me stand taller and higher, projecting my confidence to the outer world around me. It didn't alienate me from the bullying I endured in elementary school. Bullying occurs in Africa, and it's quite hard to tell whether it's as acute as what most kids face here in the Western world. Bullying made me more aware of my vulnerabilities, but not alienated from them. Dad had taught me that I could commandeer respect in life if I truly wanted. So bullying did nothing to dissipate my overall confidence as a person. Even while I walked amongst friends who were taller than me, I didn't feel extremely self-conscious or ashamed.

I can boldly say that I learned how to cultivate resilience not just because I had to face bullies but also because of my environment. A lot goes into living in an African community as a kid and a teenager. There are harsh realities in the classroom and on the home front to overcome. But in my case, they all made me grow into a better person, with a heightened understanding of what life entailed.

In our home front, my parents were the primary driving forces. They were a dynamic and formidable team. My dad is an able financial provider for both the nuclear and extended family. My mom was brave and supportive of my father every step of the way.

Like any married couple, they had disagreements and quarrels that sometimes left my mom unhappy. Still, it didn't exterminate their true commitment to each other to stay together in marriage until death came knocking for either one of them. They were rooted firmly in traditional doctrines when it came to marriage, and it helped them stick together. I'm a reflective person by nature. I usually cannot help but wonder whether modern marriages would often stick together if many of us never deviated from the traditional doctrine of marriage that is mostly universal—sticking together no matter what. Times have changed, and the scourge of divorce and separation is now worldwide due to innumerable factors. I am not writing to judge, though; I am simply writing from a place of observation and reflection.

The school was a world of its own. It was a world I liked to inhabit temporarily while growing up. My school life didn't just revolve around academics, even though I soared in it. Sports were steeped in my life as well, especially in middle school.

I barely recall having memorable friends in elementary school, but middle school and high school were different.

I remember meeting T. K. A. and B. K. D. in middle school. Life would later take us all to the University of Lome, but our friendship was built and solidified within high school and middle school walls. I believe that our combined love for sports made us naturally gravitate toward each other. Our closeness was known by our parents, teachers, schoolmates, and neighbors. We quickly got the name the Three Musketeers stamped on us because you could see us together whenever we decided to go anywhere. They were much taller than me, but height differences notwithstanding, we made a formidable team. Sometimes we hung out with other boys in our grade, and most times, it would just be the three of us. We mostly stayed out of glamorous trouble with our teachers, instead spending time on basketball courts, studying together, or engaging in fluid banter on various topics—girls included.

Looking back on it now, it wouldn't be a surprise if my friends portrayed me as some sort of a ladies' man with a wide range of expertise in the art of women. I ran my mouth about girls a lot—whom I was interested in, and whom I wasn't, whom I was playing with, how many girls I had gotten laid with—when in reality I was a virgin who never had any sexual experience nor ever had a girlfriend. I didn't even know the right words to string together, nor was I an expert on catchy phrases or interesting lines. I was comfortable talking about my imaginary relationships, and it was just that: talk.

It wasn't until I was a college freshman at the University of Lome that I had my first real girlfriend. Back then, in Lome, it wasn't a rampant practice for a boy to have a girlfriend in middle school or even high school. My father even had a clearly defined rule on the subject. The boys in the family were not allowed to have a girlfriend or even consider having a girlfriend until their high school diploma was done and dusted and they had gotten well settled in college. For my two sisters, the rules weren't as tightened. Relationship ideologies were very gender-distinctive in Africa. A woman could be ripe for marriage at an early age. So when my sisters were in high school, they could have gotten away with having boyfriends. High school was memorable for my friendships, basketball, and a bunch of other things. It was also quite memorable for my first amateurish experience with love.

In those days, our classrooms were furnished with benches, one of which was allocated to two students. I had a quiet crush on the girl who sat next to me. I never missed my classes—partly because I took my classes seriously but also partly, if I'm being honest, because of her. We shared great camaraderie even as we proceeded toward other classrooms that we shared until graduation. Of course, my feelings were kept a secret. Dad's standing rule hung above my head like a sword of Damocles, so I didn't consider it worthwhile to pursue anything serious with her. I suspect she always knew but was never going to address it because she expected I'd make the first move if I were truly interested in her. I never did.

Beyond the classroom, my friendship with T. K. D. and B. K. D. coupled with our mutual love for sports would become the primary motivations that led us to become fervent members of the neighborhood basketball team known back then simply as Bad Boys. Bad Boys was a determined and formidable team. You could see the grit and focus pulsating through the veins of the young men who played the game. The team was quite notable for participating in local tournaments too.

T. K. A. was the tallest amongst us, the one who cleared six feet. Of the three of us, he was most invested in basketball, and unsurprisingly, he excelled at it. B. K. D. and I tried our best, but our lifeblood didn't thrum the way it did in our friend. We did our best in most games, playing as well as we could, but every basketball fan knows that it's the best of the best that ultimately remains within the team. So it didn't shock us when we weren't deemed outstanding enough to continue playing the game.

It's hard to forget my time on the team anyway. My height gave me the position of a point guard. My dribbles and passes were average at best, but my brief time in Bad Boys cultivated a love for basketball within me that still hasn't dissipated to date. By the time we got to high school, our involvement started to decrease when national exams loomed. Our schoolwork increased in intensity, and so did our studies. I studied regularly with my friends, and we often chose time frames and venues for group studies. T. K. D.'s house was always the preferred choice. His mother was accommodating and welcoming, and we were always assured of plates of sumptuous meals every time we held our study groups there.

Generally, the three of us took our studies seriously, but the national exams were life-defining for every eleventh-grader in Lome. Those who were not fortunate enough to make a passing grade in all relevant subjects never proceeded to twelfth grade but were required to repeat eleventh grade for an extra year. Those who were successful enough to move on to twelfth grade would then face the baccalaureate exams at the end of twelfth grade, where they needed to pass all the subjects in the curriculum to get their high school diploma.

Most students repeated eleventh grade, but twelfth grade garnered the most repetitions. The exams were demanding and brutal. Each paper was designed to fully test the intellectual prowess of each student to determine if they deserved to be bestowed with a diploma. So it wasn't surprising to see others repeat the twelfth grade two or three times. For me, repeating was an academic abomination. The thought alone was chilling to the bone. It wasn't in any way an option to even be on the precipice, so I studied hard. The hours of group study paid off, and the Three Musketeers passed the baccalaureate exams in one sitting, making it to college in a timely fashion.

Life took us through different pathways as we majored in different courses and hung out less often. I have never forgotten them because it was with those guys that I first felt a kinship close to brotherhood outside the family. They defined what friendship was to me in more ways than one.

I think I owe my academic success not just to my dad's inspiration but also to my intellectual curiosity, sparked by one teacher in particular. I'll call him Mr. A. He was our philosophy teacher in twelfth grade. I had gone through many teachers in twelfth grade. Still, Mr. A stood out for his easy ability to deconstruct the familiar, engage us in critical thinking, and stimulate our young minds to think and reflect beyond things we perceive as factual. Getting young minds to do this in any part of the world is difficult, but he got us to do it. He opened the ballast of my mind to a new dimension, and in several ways, it still serves me to date. I'll always remember his voice discussing Descartes's philosophy, booming through the class, saying, "I think therefore I am." They were the five words that constructed the bridge that took me from a high school academic star to a critical thinker.

I have tried to discuss my childhood as extensively as I can. Immigration didn't come through until after I completed college, and I intend to discuss the full immigration story in the third chapter. The backstory is pretty simple. Lome didn't offer enough opportunities for the type of success I truly craved, even though I was armed with a university degree and a master's in management. It isn't unusual that Lome offered very few opportunities. The systems in place were insufficient to handle the sheer number of annual graduates. The entire country has just two universities. At the time I graduated, the country had just one.

The hardship that engulfed me due to the high unemployment rate led me to take on a pitiful job as a teacher in a private business school. I was there until I became sickened with the lack of hope, the peanut salary, and the apparent lack of proper systems, which could never guarantee my success. It had never been in my dreams before this period to leave my home country. I loved Lome, and it took so much to entertain the thought of leaving, of going to a foreign land. But the stark reality of my alternatives left me with no real choices. The thought had always stayed tightly locked in my subconscious that there were many divergent angles to attain success. First, one had to find his niche. It could be creative or athletic endeavors. It could be scholarly or linguistic intelligence, business ventures, or a lifetime career. For me, I was simply inspired by Dad. I wanted to be admired and respected for the content of my brain. Knowledge was, to me, a hidden treasure I had to keep seeking. I decided to leave Lome for the United States, where I believed my dreams of a better life would converge into a glorious reality, and I became the first in my family to do so—to conquer the unknown by reinventing myself in a different time and place.

Preceding all this, however, was college at the University of Lome. If allowed, I could relive the first and one true experience a thousand times. My college voyage was simply a continuation of my endless search for knowledge. The minute my high school diploma was in my hands, I proclaimed that I was on my way to appropriating myself with what money couldn't buy.

CHAPTER 2

The African College Life

College was an amazing time. I consider it one of the best periods in my adult life. I consider it a time when I started to come into my own. College was the first place where I first tasted true freedom. When I got into college, my parents stopped ordering me and lessened their grip on their control. They shared their perspectives with me on certain issues, equating me as an adult and not a child. In college, education felt incredibly different. It started to feel more connected to my future and what I had envisioned for my life. It was in college that I also got a first taste of what relevance is and how it feels. Back then, in the university, the students felt the valuable knowledge that they carried their nation's leadership and intellectual future on their shoulders. Maybe it's a great responsibility, but it is the kind of responsibility that gives great relevance, a relevance that stays undiminished for a long time. College was crucial in so many ways. It was a period of evolving into maturity and responsibility, a period where one makes decisions that eventually come to shape their adult life.

Before my debut into college life happened, I was afflicted by a series of political events that affected my education and the total educational system in Togo.

The series of events began in 1990 and led to a general strike of an indefinite period launched in November 1992, which caused the loss of a full school year at all levels of the education system. In fact, it all started with short strikes by students at the University of Lome to claim improvements in their living conditions. These strikes were followed by arrests and torture of students, which led to the creation of a human rights league and student activist associations. Because student strikes were severely and brutally repressed, a group of mothers took to the streets of Lome to protest against the mistreatment of their children. That year, one thing led to another: a strike by taxi drivers, a strike against rising prices, a nationwide curfew, and finally, a tragedy. Twenty-eight bodies, including two pregnant women and one with a child on her back, were found in a lagoon in a district of Lome called Bè. The visual image is still in my head to date. I shuddered the first time I saw them, shaken to my deepest cores that emanated from the brutalities that had come to characterize our nation at that point.

In July of the same year, the Togolese people decided to hold a national conference to discuss the future of their country and to forgive each other, but the project ended in a fishtail. The governing political power abruptly put an end to the process. Consequently, a general strike of an indefinite period was launched in November 1992 by the political opposition to demand respect for democracy. As a result, the 1992–1993 school year was a lost year, and like many hundreds of thousands of young Togolese at the time, I was not in school all year. I should have completed my senior year of high school that year, but since there was an indefinite strike in place, and schools were closed in Lome and a large portion of the territory, I spent the academic year doing extracurricular activities.

At that time, the capital city of Lome was the hot spot for political violence, so my father made the decision to send the family to his village, where things were totally peaceful. During the months I spent in his village along with my mother and siblings, I got the opportunity to learn more about rural life. I also met cousins whom I did not know before.

To escape our boredom and make good use of our free time at hand away from school, we decided to start a cultural association, which included both the many young folks returning to the village from Lome for safety and the local teenagers. We ended up learning songs and plays that we regularly performed at a cultural center in the village and in a nearby town. As part of our association, I initiated the creation of a karate group, which performed self-defense techniques and forms to the delight of the villagers during the association's events. In a way, these extracurricular activities while in refuge in my paternal village built unexpected and everlasting joyous memories during a dark time in my country's history.

Those memorable times in the village unlocked an innate appreciation for rural life. It was like a throwback to our ingrained culture that the Europeans tried to wipe out by promoting the false narrative that Africa had no culture. Cultural relevance and the love for it are still lacking within the African continent due to a substantial shortage of the true spirit of Pan-Africanism.

With regard to the political turmoil and instability that affected my life back then in Togo, it's saddening to note that such things are still prominent on the continent as a whole. As a child, none of the things that happened in the political sphere of the nation really registered with me. As I became older, I started to become aware of how much influence the government wielded over the most mundane aspects of the common man's existence. Although there are plenty of beautiful and successful stories about life in Africa, if I'm being honest, the lack of opportunity for many remains one main motivating factor for leaving the shores of many of its countries. This is leading to a large-scale, worrisome happening called brain drain. How exactly is development supposed to occur with so much brain drain happening? I wonder about this, but I have no answers.

I still believe that politics is a profound force that can be used for great change with the right principles and the right person holding the reins. But sometimes, these things are more deeply rooted and complex than that. Eventually, my transition to college occurred. The evolution wielded power over my joys and worries. And there were things to be worried about.

The first was money. Dad handled my college fees. He also did his best to always provide what was necessary. Still, under the weight of his financial responsibility, it wasn't always easy to get everything requested, and I knew why. The tuition fees in Togo back then were not expensive. A rough annual calculation of everything amassed to about two hundred dollars in today's American currency. Now, two hundred dollars for a college education might seem affordable, especially compared to what is being paid here for college fees, but back then, it didn't feel affordable. For many low-income families living in rural areas, paying two hundred dollars yearly was painstaking. For them, poverty was ruthless—a large-scale societal problem that walked on two legs.

One of the ways I tried to make extra money on my own was by becoming a tutor. I started in high school and continued into my college years. Becoming a tutor was easy. All it required was a walk around the neighborhood, making inquiries from the families by asking if their middle school or high school child needed someone to come in and help with their schoolwork. If the family agrees, the potential tutor negotiates their price and structured daily hours. The market was there; all it required was to sell yourself and your skills. Of course, the money wasn't huge because these families were less privileged for the most part, but it helped sort out some personal bills, which was the most important thing.

In America, students can hold part-time jobs while attending college. Part-time jobs did not exist in my home country. Tutoring was the one thing that came close. Tutoring, though, was more than just a job for me. I felt a sense of responsibility toward the students I tutored. For me, it felt as though a significant amount of their academic success was largely dependent upon me and my teaching style, so I took it pretty seriously.

Most of the students I was fortunate to tutor were students struggling at school. Nevertheless, I had a few students who were remarkably bright to the point that it felt as if their parents were wasting their money by hiring me. Well, I sure did not complain about it since I needed the job to make my own living. Still, I invested heavily in these remarkably bright kids to make them learn beyond their grade level. I vividly remember two middle schoolers I was hired to tutor in mathematics, chemistry, and physics. They were quite interesting in many ways: they seemed to be the human representation of the yin and yang. Their parents were an upper-middle-class couple, a medical doctor married to a lawyer. Medical doctors and lawyers are professions back home that guarantee a decent living. It's still true to date.

At that time, I was a senior in high school. The two middle schoolers were twin brothers. One was very bright, the other not so bright. Their parents did not want to hire a tutor for just the not-so-bright kid so that he would not feel embarrassed and extra self-conscious, two factors that could lead to unnecessary self-esteem issues. So both became my tutored students.

What was striking about them was the fact that they were identical twins. At first, that distracted me and made it hard to get their names right, especially because they would dress alike in the same color. They occasionally reveled in the mystery of their identical looks, and oftentimes they engaged in reckless mischief. I discovered this one day when they jointly decided to trick me.

It's a long story, but to make the long story short, I went over a chemistry lesson with them during a prior meeting and informed them that I would be testing them separately at our next meeting. So on that day, in the study room in their home, I asked the first brother to solve a chemistry equation on the medium-sized movable blackboard conveniently installed in the study room by their parents. As you rightfully guessed, yes, we were at the age of white chalk and blackboard.

When the first brother was working on my chemistry assignment, I asked the other twin brother to wait outside the room for his turn. A couple of minutes later, when the other twin brother came in to solve the same chemistry equation, the first brother took his spot outside. They both did amazingly well on the assignment, so I was delighted that the lesson was mastered. We could move on to other chapters. A few days later, their parents informed me that one of the twins, the not-so-bright kid, did very poorly on a test from school about solving the same chemistry equation.

Naturally, I was confused. It turned out that the day I had them solve the equation separately so that I could see if either of them still needed extra help with the lesson, the first twin who solved my assignment in the study room was the same twin who returned to the study room, instead of his twin brother, to brilliantly solve the assignment again. That day, as on many other days, they'd dressed alike in the same color, and I was fooled by their trick. Their parents were very upset when they figured out their deception. I was not actually upset but pensively amused by the fact that I fell for it.

That day was the last time I saw them dressed alike. Their parents decided, moving forward, to have them wear different clothing in different colors. And the grades of the not-so-bright twin improved over time, just enough to pass his two most challenging classes: mathematics and physics. It was an interesting and unique tutoring experience because of the fact that the two students were identical twins with opposite aptitudes for the scientific courses. The bright twin brother always scored the highest grade on all his tests at school. His twin was actually also bright in most courses—such as languages, history, and drawing—but had serious difficulties in STEM-related classes.

At the beginning of my tutoring, I had a twice-a-week schedule with them. After their unfortunate trickery and the very bad grade in chemistry by the not-so-bright twin, I agreed to change my schedule to three times a week, which led to more work and, naturally, an increase in my modest salary. In the end, as was the case in most of my tutoring experiences while in high school and college, the twins ended up getting their high school diplomas a few years later, and I heard that their parents sent them to France for college. I often wonder about them. Mostly I wonder about how they are doing, what they are doing, and if they still trick innocent folks with their identical looks.

The second thing to worry about was freshman year. There was a limited-seat nightmare that prevailed in the first year of the School of Business. With all the high school students in Togo gunning to get themselves admitted into the University of Lome, which was, at that time, the only university in the country, the university itself had to implement certain rules in certain departments in order not to become overwhelmed.

The University of Lome was a world of its own. During my time, it had a twelve thousand-student population divided into several faculties with many departments in the fields of business, economics, law, languages, engineering, sociology, medicine, pharmacy, engineering, communication, philosophy, anthropology, mathematics, physics, chemistry, and biology.

The School of Business was nicknamed Popular China because of how prominent it was and how many students were enrolled annually. During my time, we were 2,500 freshmen enrolled in the school of business. And that's a large number.

The School of Business was the largest department on campus, yet there were limited staff and limited facilities, and it could only handle a restricted number of students. So it implemented a rule that required the freshmen to fight for their spot amid the insufficient facilities. The rule was this: For a freshman to become a sophomore, they had to not only score a passing grade but also be among the highest five hundred passing grades. For context, we were 2,500 students in the freshman year, but only five hundred spots were available in the sophomore year. What did this mean? It meant that 2,500 students had come to the School of Business with their dreams, but two thousand of them would see those dreams squashed. Back then, clearly, education wasn't a right.

The rule only applied to the freshman year. From the sophomore year upward, there were no more limited seats as long as students managed to pass a set of courses at that level. So of course, during freshman year, my sole focus was to become a part of the top five hundred and avoid being bagged and tagged with the remaining two thousand who had to forgo their dreams of getting a business degree. Forgoing my dreams was not an option for me.

Since Togo now has two universities, I am unsure whether this practice has been discontinued or still in place. However, most African countries retain certain strategies in higher institutions due to limited facilities that are not commensurate with the sheer number of students who long for a college education. In all parts of an African system, there are usually insufficient resources, and I have come to realize that lack breeds a competitive mindset. This is why competitions are set up with the aim of colossal failure, so that the system manages to breathe for a limited period. It is, in my opinion, an unfortunate way of life. Nonetheless, it is brutal reality.

I had always found academics easy, but freshman academics did not strike me as easy because it wasn't just enough to pass. I incorporated a twofold study strategy in my freshman year so the system wouldn't beat me; instead, I would beat it. First, I did my best to pay rapt attention in class and subconsciously memorized the lessons until I knew them by heart. Then

I would sit with three friends and we would revise past questions from previous years. This helped us to consciously build the knowledge required to fully comprehend the subject matter and to be familiar with the kinds of questions the professors could throw at us in the exam hall. The strategies worked because when we did take the exams, and the results were pasted for all to see, I ranked number 4 in the top five hundred freshmen of the school of business. This was my first defining moment post-high school. I still consider it one of my best achievements within the walls of the University of Lome. I remember beaming as I saw my name on the board by the number 4. I also remember thinking, " Kodjo, it can only get easier for you from here onward." Maybe I was right, but I was only right in the academic sphere. The rest of my academic years at Lome were a breeze.

Of course, this doesn't mean that college was easy. Far from it. Often I cannot help but wonder how different life would have been if Western educational executions were available back then for us in Lome. The university had a lot of disadvantages. We had to make do with scarce amenities. The concept of free internet was simply nonexistent. Want to use the internet? Great! Pay per minute for whatever you want to use.

There was a severe deficiency in student bus transportation. Most of us would either pitch money together to ply in a costly taxi or take ourselves on a two-hour walk because, on most days, buses to college were unavailable. And finding a student with a personal car was as rare as finding real pure gold lying carelessly on the streets. Even most of our parents and professors didn't own cars. The most fortunate students owned motor scooters, or mopeds. It was easy to envy their privilege after a tiring two-hour-long walk, not in an ill-spirited fashion, just an ingrained admiration of the lucky minority.

Walking was naturally infused into our lives. In our neighborhood, people often walked to shops, workplaces, and schools for thirty to forty minutes. I often rode in a taxi with my friends to a neighborhood close to mine. And by *close*, I mean the taxi saved me just one hour of trekking or an hour and thirty minutes in some lucky cases. Then I would continue my legwork toward my home. It was the norm back then, and many of us became used to it.

There was also nothing like a university library, where anyone could go to borrow books. That concept, too, was nonexistent. When we needed books that matched the curriculum, we'd saunter toward the shelves of street booksellers and check out what they had. Going through college as a student, I rarely had my textbooks.

Accommodation facilities were really limited as well. During my time at the University of Lome, there were two dormitories on campus, one for female students and one for male students. Each dormitory had fewer than two hundred beds. Since a few thousand students would request a room in a dormitory, generally, priorities were understandably given to students who graduated from cities and towns outside the capital city of Lome, but some students from Lome managed to get a room. For most of us who grew up in Lome, because our families resided in Lome, even if not within the proximity of the campus, we simply commuted from our distant neighborhood. I'm thankful for those times because they afforded me more time and space with friends and family as opposed to sharing a small room with a bunch of strangers. Back then, I definitely did not see it as a disadvantage.

From the news I received last year, the number of dormitories has increased to six in recent years. That is certainly a step in the right direction. Many other improvements have taken shape. The total enrolment at the University of Lome has also increased significantly to a whooping sixty thousand students last year compared to only twelve thousand when I attended. The country shall definitely invest in building a few more public universities to meet the tangible demand of its growing student population. Of course, the hope is that job-creation initiatives shall follow accordingly. I'm grateful whenever I hear things like this that signify growth and a profound upward trajectory. There's always going to be hope for my people.

Back in those days, we copied long notes directly from the blackboard written with white chalk. Our professors would take hours to copy long notes on the boards, and we would, in turn, take hours to copy the content of courses in our notes. We copied word for word, sentence by sentence, formula by formula, and drawings. By the time the semester ended, many of us had hundreds of pages filled with inky notes per course. Exceptions were only made when professors had paper photocopies of parts of the course, which were always sold to us for a fee.

Our exams took place at the end of the semester, and grades were posted publicly. Grade confidentiality was not in any way a thing. Final semester exam results were posted on bulletin boards outside each department for everyone to see. A bad grade was a bad grade, a good grade was a good grade, and it remained that way, end of story. There were no syllabi or grading criteria back then, so students were often unfairly graded and dissatisfied with a grade they got. There are times as a student when you would study hard, write an exam, and be confident that you have aced it until the unbelievable results were out. It was common to have a faster heartbeat and a sinking heart whenever you saw your grades.

Contrary to what I have witnessed in America, our professors were treated and revered like kings and queens. The concept of a written evaluation by students, which is, in reality, an overall assessment of their professors, sounded so foreign and alien to me when I first heard about it. Admirable, yes, but still downright weird and somewhat amusing. I bet it never even occurred to the mind of anyone back then in Lome to implement such. The concept of FERPA (Family Educational Rights Privacy Act) in America would have caused my professors in school back then to screech with bellyaching and teary laughter. Nevertheless, I understand the implementation of the act and its use. It is just one of the many things that define the ideological differences prominent between the first and third worlds. Distinctive environments are characterized by specific challenges, different realities, and different survival mechanisms.

The fact that our university professors were revered as kings and queens and people not to mess with kept us at a considerable distance in terms of the relationship between them and us. For the most part, our relationship with them was limited to the time we saw them teaching in our crowded amphitheaters and classrooms. I did not know of any professors who shared their office hours. Most of them did not have their own office to begin with. Therefore, an opportunity for a one-on-one connection was almost nonexistent for many students. However, that changed in my junior year when I became the representative of students in the School of Business.

That year there was a young newly hired professor called Dr. K. L. L. who, we later learned, studied at Howard University in the United States. His way of approaching students was refreshingly different. He was very approachable and even cracked jokes with us during class. He was easygoing, not showing off as most of his senior colleagues in the department, attentive to our needs, and actually invested in us as learners.

In my role as representative, I was fortunate to meet with our professors to talk about various issues or to simply relay information to my classmates from them. This was how I got close to Professor K. L. L. With the other professors, it was totally different; it was the strict servant-and-boss dynamic and nothing more. They didn't pretend to be friends, and I didn't pretend to be more than a student representative. With Professor K. L. L., things were vastly different. Our prolonged interactions quickly veered into an older brother–to–younger brother relationship. I would fairly say that he was the closest thing to a mentor that I experienced during my college years in Togo. And inevitably, he became my favorite professor.

He would happily share anecdotes and stories of his time at Howard University in Washington, DC, with me, one of which I still remember to date. It was a funny story. To the best of my recollection, he was recounting the fate of an African friend of his who had newly migrated to Washington, DC, when he was still there, and the friend got lost in the streets. The story goes like this:

He and his friend, along with others, were out doing errands when the said friend, physically tired of walking too long, decided to leave the group and return to their shared apartment building down a few blocks. The irony was that many of the buildings were characterized by a sameness that made them difficult to identify.

So on his journey back to the apartment, this friend suddenly realized that he did not know the building number nor the cell phone number of any of the friends he'd left moments ago. The group was already out of sight, and he was unwilling to turn back, so he trusted his guts and bravely proceeded to continue the pursuit of identifying his apartment. A few hours later, he was still looking, finding himself at times in the wrong building that looked like his. In the meantime, his friends had returned to the shared apartment and were surprised by his absence. And as his prolonged absence became worrisome to all, they had no choice but to look for him.

The building had two entrances: one at the front and one in the back. Professor K. L. L. and another friend exited the building through the back entrance while the remaining friends walked out the front door. As soon as Professor K. L. L. and his friend exited the building, they saw their lost friend seated on a bench across the street in silent tears of desperation. It was quite a surprise. What happened was the lost friend did not know that he was actually staring at the back of his own building. He was only familiar with the front design of the building.

Well, all was well that ended well. One can only imagine the laughter and jokes that were shared that evening among these friends when they reunited minutes later in the comfort of their shared apartment and brotherhood. That dramatic yet hilarious story clearly survived the passage of time. One singular testimony of that is me sharing it here with you.

When I left Togo after my graduation, Professor K. L. L. was still teaching at the University of Lome, mentoring and enlightening the lives and dreams of many who came after me. A few years ago, I learned that after twenty years of service to the University of Lome, he decided to settle in Canada, and we reconnected via LinkedIn. What a small world!

I admired Professor K. L. L. for his easygoing attitude and the rare passion the man possessed for teaching. Back then, at the University of Lome, he was like a unicorn. He didn't have to be nice to us. He could have chosen to be just as arrogant and super strict as the other professors and just as high-minded, but he wasn't. From him, I learned about the power of choice. It's very much possible to be who you want and what you want.

No doubt we had so many struggles we all had to contend with going through college in Lome. These days, things are better for the average contemporary student. They might still face challenges because college is not naturally a problem-free experience, but situations definitely tend to get better with time. For those of us from the past generation, these were the disadvantages and hurdles the flawed system wreaked on us. It made us stronger and more determined to graduate with good grades. After all, what was the point of all those impediments if we didn't graduate with respectable grades?

Everything I have outlined made college memorable. Living in Lome as a whole bred the first tendrils of the resilience that would come to characterize my life, but I'd say college takes the lion's share of that breeding. What made college delightfully interesting, though, were the relationships I managed to cultivate. I made many beautiful friends who gave me many special and unforgettable memories I still cherish to this day.

Friendships were the cushions that ameliorated whatever pain or frustrations college might have been putting us through regarding the grading system and the considerable lack of amenities.

I spent joyful times with my friends in school and on summer vacations. I spent my free time hanging out with three of my closest friends, T. A. A., A. F., and Brother R. I studied regularly with them and worked together as a group when we were undergraduates. I still keep in touch with them.

T. A. A. lives and works in Canada in the banking sphere. A. F. now works as a management professor in Togo, and Brother R. left our business field for the Catholic Church, where he serves God as a priest. Back then, none of us knew the different paths life would take us. We defined our futures while we created memories in the present.

Whenever we completed our group study sessions, the four of us would go out to chill on the streets of Nyekonakpoe, which was within walking distance from our homes. Most street vendors arrived in the early evenings to set up their businesses, hoping to catch the attention of those coming from work or school like us. My friends and I frequently patronized a lady who sold donuts and corn porridge. It was our local treat, the one we would give ourselves after long hours of study sessions. We would eat, chat, crack jokes, say hi to passersby, and just unwind. Those were when we did not have to think about our futures or circumstances. During those languorous evenings, we lived in the moment.

During one of those carefree evenings during my freshman year, I came in contact with my first girlfriend. I'll call her N. C. She passed by that evening and stopped to say hi to T. A.

A. The first thing that struck me about her was her profound beauty. She gave a shy smile, and I was smitten at once. Her walking steps were unreal, with magical flawlessness to them. And her eyes? They were striking and attractive, as though she were a princess from a fairy tale. I stared shamelessly at her that day, trying to quell my fast heartbeat. After her brief greetings to my friend, she went on her way. The second she was gone, I pounced on him immediately. Who was she? How did he know her? Where did she live? Did she have a boyfriend? T. A. A. laughed, but luckily for me, he knew her quite well and agreed to make an introduction. He initiated our first meeting and, subsequently, our first date. Shortly after that, she became my girlfriend.

My very first. We were both young virgins, but our relationship thrived and was wonderful during its one-year time frame. Her mother never approved of me because someone from my extended family, it seemed, had once disappointed a woman from her extended family. It was like a long tapestry of family complexities that we believed were not much of our concern, so we jointly fought her mother's pressure for as long as we could. But in the end, she gave in. I won't deny that letting her go was painful. It was my first brush with heartbreak. Thankfully, I had my friends who always tried to cheer and uplift my spirits as well as my grand entrance into the sophomore year from my applaudable number 4 position. In no time, my heart healed up.

Beyond my buddies, my social school life extended to spending time with my cousins. I was remarkably close to one in particular—A. W. D. She and I were born the same year, so within our extended family, we were known as twins. She attended the same business school at the University of

Lome, but her family lived far away from mine, so she was in a different study group closer to home. Nevertheless, we were always tight. We visited each other often and shared our fears, secrets, and plans for the future. We supported each other in various endeavors, and her beauty gained the admiration of several of my male friends. However, none of them could measure up in a religious sense because she was a committed Jehovah's Witness.

College might have had its challenges, but it was nonetheless great fun. It was a world in its own right, and I basked in it. It was an alternate world from the one I had grown up in, which had been strictly pervaded by my family. An insane level of freedom, joyous and humorous moments, and exposure to an exponential level of hard work that fine-tuned and molded me. I learned to be a true believer in love, friendship, and resilience.

Graduation was my second defining moment. For the five hundred of us who made it to sophomore year in the School of Business, our final graduation three years later bestowed upon us our bachelor's degrees, then master's degrees, and caused much happiness among our family and friends, leading to a string of joyful celebrations. Back then, we didn't have ceremonies the way we have them now. You graduated the minute you checked out your last set of results on the bulletin board. The next stage was to kick-start a career because the university did not have a doctoral program. And so, in the year 1999, I received a master of sciences in management degree from the University of Lome.

After the joy of graduation wore off, it was time to face the grim reality of my situation. The unemployment rate was incredibly high. So high that even my polished education wasn't sufficient to escape becoming a second-class citizen in my home country. The minute I graduated was my official initiation into adulthood. My father had trained me and done his best. However, I was left to become my own man, and the system was not smiling at me. Adulthood came with its problems and trials, many of which I was grossly unprepared for.

Chapter **3**

Audacity of Migrating

Humans, despite their limitations, are naturally audacious. If we are being one-hundred-percent honest, many of us believe that we have the trajectories of our lives and maybe even our destinies mapped out. We strategize plans, ideas, dreams, and goals for our lives even when we have seen or have been told that life is highly unpredictable. We try to put our set agendas in motion, and when life hits us unpredictably, we wonder what is happening.

There is a lot of audacity in that.

But then what are we to do? It is foolish to leave your life vulnerable to twists of fate. You always have to take charge of it and stay fully in control. This is what I have always believed in. It is how I operate even up until this day. We all need to have a mind of our own. It is audacious, but audacity breeds tenacity. Tenacity, in return, builds resilience. After I finished my bachelor's degree and master's in management from the University of Lome, I was confronted with the harsh reality of a brutally inept system that had the power to rob me of the bright future I had always wanted for my life. Unemployment descended on me like a ton of bricks.

No matter where I turned, there were no proper jobs despite my hard-earned degrees. The problem was that I was just one in a thousand brilliant and talented folks who also wanted bright futures and had impressive and formidable degrees. We erroneously believed they would secure our future in a country starved of hope, steeped in stagnancy, and drowned in past regrets. Instead of living our glorious dreams, surviving became the number 1 prerogative. It was disheartening and slightly amusing to see graduates drive what was known as *Zemidjan*, in a future where the possibility of driving public transportation had never been conceived. Zemidjan was a means of transportation, a taxi-moto, that achieved mainstream popularity in Lome but was an actual innovation of Benin— our neighboring country. This mode of transportation was used to move through major roads that were often too busy to navigate. The scourge of unemployment was endemic. Survival was a daily endeavor. It became the lifeblood by which most graduates lived and thrived—like a vicious perpetual cycle of nowhere.

During the first six months post-graduation, I applied for jobs, searching high and low as desperately as I could. I even went to the point of taking my résumé to a few store owners in the largest open market looking for an entry-level administrative position, all to no avail. Yet giving up hope was not an option. I would wake up every morning determined and armed to the teeth with my qualifications and in my moderately decent corporate clothes. Most afternoons I would be back dampened by hope in the sweltering heat, my throat parched with thirst and bitterness. But eventually, it all paid off. At least a little bit for a little while.

Finally, I was hired for a three-month internship at a major bank in Lome. I still recall seeing the appointment letter. At that moment, hope rushed in, knocking at my door. I was delighted. I tried to convince myself that all I needed to do was perform well during my internship, and before I knew it, a permanent employment contract would land on my desk and I would become a banker. I'd take care of my folks, make enough money to make ends meet, and build a better life for myself. So I determinedly dedicated myself to the bank. The first thing I took care of was to invest my light savings into buying new ties to look sharp and professional. Most bank employees dressed very sharply. I wanted to fit in, and I did. Well, at least that was my impression.

I never showed up late. I volunteered on several occasions to work beyond my regular hours. My supervisor, kind and gentle by nature, would not allow me to work overtime. It was, as he said, company policy with interns. My work itself was not sophisticated. What I do recall was that it was not related to any course I took during my undergraduate and graduate studies at the School of Business. Nevertheless, my degrees prepared me to quickly grasp the practical banking concepts to which I was introduced and meet my daily performance expectations. Time flew by fast. The third month saw me feeling almost like a member of the bank family. I got accustomed to most employees on my floor. They were nice to me, professional, and encouraging. They also began to call me by my first name. The future seemed to be taking shape, with an inevitably bright outcome. At that point, I ventured into researching the salary range I could expect at the entry level should I be hired. The dreams continued unabated. In fact, in the deepest recesses of my mind, they began to expand: build my future house, start a family, climb the professional ladder, coach young interns in my turn years from there, and many more. As the saying goes, "I built castles in Spain." One week before the end of my internship, an official letter sealed in an immaculate envelope was given to me.

The leadership of the bank was thanking me for my wonderful performance during my internship and wishing me all the best in my endeavors at the conclusion of my three-month contract. They added that I have qualities that will assure a bright professional career when I start one.

"Okay, that's nice, but why then let me go?" I murmured to myself.

No permanent position was offered to me. And that had always been the dream and the expectation. They constantly hire interns, and clearly, they could not offer them all a permanent position. On that day, standing on the ground floor of the bank and reading the paper as I was wracked with disbelief, the dream ended right there and then crashed like a stack of cards. It felt painful, but I quickly got back to my senses. I was grateful for the opportunity. Some of my schoolmates who graduated with me did not find one internship. I decided to remain optimistic.

A few months later, I found another internship, in the cabinet of a certified public accountant. This time, it was only for one month. I had started it hopeful and optimistic, but within a few days, my optimism was dampened. The experience was awful. I did not learn much. My daily task was going through tons of files and reclassifying them according to some metrics I was shown. It quickly became boring. I would impatiently wait for closing so I could dash home. And as the days started to feel like weeks, they became unsustainable. No concrete accounting operation ever crossed my desk so that I could gain any practical experience. To worsen the nightmare, I was later tasked to compare numbers on duplicate sheets and cross out repeated numbers. When I asked what the numbers represented, I was politely told not to bother about it. There I had it—I was an office clerk. Nothing wrong with being an office clerk, but I needed something more. I felt no regret when the one-month contract came to an end. I was actually relieved.

A few months later, still no job interview was in sight, although my résumé at that point had reached some human resource offices twice. In my neighborhood, a newly opened private business school was looking for instructors in general economics. I thanked the gods for the timing of such an appealing opportunity. I was hired as soon as I sent my résumé. There I was, feeling glorious. I was about to be a general economics professor. I could envision myself inspiring the next generation of savvy financial leaders, business owners, and monetary policymakers. Yes, my teaching was going to have an impact. I truly believed it.

The beginning of the new semester was just around the corner when I was hired. So when I met with the director of that private business school to discuss my salary, it was the day before the first day of classes. I even went to the meeting with the first few chapters I had already prepared, displaying the utmost enthusiasm for the opportunity. I had a fair idea about how much professors of general economics, who possessed master's degrees, were making at equivalent public schools. And since this institution was a private one, it made sense in my mind that the salary would automatically be higher. Nonetheless,

I was prepared to accept a slightly lower salary in the worst-case scenario, I told myself.

What I was offered was beneath peanuts. It was the equivalent of what I was paid as a tutor when I was still in high school. It felt like an unbelievably cruel joke. I thought the director was just introducing me to his sense of humor. That was not the case. I stared at him and saw the seriousness in his eyes. It was revolting. What was I to do? Stand up and leave? Send him to hell? Kick his buttocks and slam the doors in rage? I kept calm instead. The salary bar was ridiculously low. To date, I still can't even articulate my disappointment. That was how much the other professors were getting paid. I swallowed my wounded pride and showed up to class the next day.

The students were adorable, attentive, and eager to learn. I did my part and met them with enthusiasm and the commitment expected from me. Every time I would see the director in the hallway or the schoolyard, my stomach would start turning up. The tuition the students paid was higher than the average. But my peanut salary could barely afford one decent shirt and one decent pair of pants. This was when my reflections about my future began to take a new turn. Migration started coming to mind.

The peanut salary made me depressed, and I knew that if I didn't do something, I would be caught up in that vicious haze of nothingness and despair. I hated my circumstances and didn't want to hate my life, stewing in the bitterness and resentment I felt toward the powers that had designed, organized, and orchestrated my frustration. I've never been one to dwell on my problems or dwell on what causes them. What is the solution? There's always a solution.

After much thought and rumination, I decided that leaving the borders of my country was the best decision at that time. Living outside Lome would expose me to better opportunities and propel me to a much bigger leverage point. The velocity of that decision made me feel empowered then, but I was also filled with trepidation.

Life in the vast unknown is always like that. The terrain is always riddled with fear. I was even more fearful because no sibling in my nuclear family had ever done this. I would be the pioneer. It did feel like a call of destiny, and I decided I would answer. I knew the road ahead would be paved with difficulty. I anticipated the loneliness I would feel without the warmth and comfort of my family after a long day of work and deep soul-searching. I knew I would no longer be able to eat the sweet, homely cooking of my beloved mother or the masculine company of my father and brothers.

I knew I would not see my friends from college and the neighborhood, coupled with my extended family members, for a long time. My everyday life would be altered considerably. I would not wake up to the tropical sun or the sound of the singing birds. My life as I knew it would change completely. I imagined myself walking alone, locked in a perpetual conflict with who I was, with my African worldviews and perceptions, in opposition to who my new environment expected me to be, and then forced by the unknown to question my identity and overall existence. Yet I knew I had to leave. I had to forget it all if I wanted to broaden the dimensions of my reality. Taking my life up a notch was much more important. I still recall the look on my father's face when I told him I wanted to travel overseas.

"You want to leave?"

I nodded with conviction. "Yes."

"Have you thought about it?"

"I have, and I believe I have better prospects over there."

My father was silent for so long that I thought he might disagree. Then he uttered words that would make me love him even more deeply than before. "I will support you."

As I smiled and expressed my appreciation, I saw a different kind of respect slip into his eyes. A quiet admiration. He didn't just respect my decision; he was proud of the man I was becoming. He was grateful that I understood that my life was solely in my hands and that I was smart enough to change trajectory since Lome did not offer many prospects then.

My father supported me by getting me a loan that was on a two-year repayment plan. This loan was instrumental in getting me to the States, and even though it is paid back in full, I can never forget his trust and faith on my behalf. Reflecting upon it now, I realize my father could have repaid the loan. Still, in my opinion, he wanted to teach me an important parenting lesson that allowed me to develop a proper sense of responsibility and cultivate a reasonable level of discipline. His parenting lesson was monumentally helpful. I learned to be self-sufficient and independent, and I have never turned to anyone in the United States or at home for a loan to date. I learned to live within my means and weather my self-imposed financial restrictions.

Getting a visa back then was such a struggle that if you did manage to get one, it was a good accomplishment that would always trigger a celebration. It's ironic, isn't it? Foreigners have no issues crossing borders and sauntering easily into our own countries. Most African embassies do not even inquire about the prerequisite visa before granting access. On the other hand, the restrictions that characterize the frontiers of Western countries are colossal. It seems that they become even stricter and tougher as time goes by. It's sadly ironic and says a lot about power dynamics and equality in today's world.

Leaving Lome was a grand affair. January 10, 2001, was an unforgettable day in my mind's eye. To date, I can still see my family and friends clearly, numbering up to about twenty, coming to wish me heartfelt farewells and good wishes.

Their presence comforted me and temporarily relinquished my fears. I became very appreciative of the moment, savoring it for as long as I could. Hours later, as I sat on my seat by the window side of the plane, looking down at what remained of my old life and waiting to be propelled to the new one, fear solidified into an iron resolution that remains undiminished even today. I would define my destiny, build my dreams with my two hands, and make my family and friends immensely proud. My new quest would not be fruitless and regrettable. I had never wanted to leave my friends and family, yet I wanted to leave Togo and live a life where the margins were determined by me and me alone. Not a system.

Over the years, many of my college friends made the same decision to define their destinies in foreign lands. Unfortunately, only a handful of them survived the test of time and distance. To date, I communicate fairly well with a bunch of them, and I am truly grateful for what we have built and preserved and how it remains unshakable. It's hard to tell the exact number of those who did migrate as I did. Still, as social media flourished, I learned or heard from a few who settled in Europe and North America or those who moved to other African countries like Senegal, Ivory Coast, and Burkina Faso. Of course, we are all grownups now with different lives, priorities, responsibilities, and careers. These days, keeping in touch for a long period is hard, so we are left with shorter time frames. Life has taken us through different pathways. As we say in Africa, "Twenty children cannot play together for twenty years."

Flying was a first-time experience, but it was wonderful, and I have loved it ever since. I landed at the Baltimore Washington International Airport on January 11, 2001, dressed laughably as a Miami tourist. The biting-cold winter was a revelation. The cold alarmed me, and it would take years before I eventually learned to adapt and let go of the sunny tropical weather of Togo. I like winters for the beauty of pearly white glistening snow, but I have never truly adjusted to snowstorms or the slippery roads that make driving a bit more complex.

Upon my arrival in Baltimore, I stayed a few months with my cousin M. A. He was kind, good-natured, and friendly, with a firm reed of integrity within him. We got along incredibly well. He was easy to like and easy to talk to. Cousin M. A. and I have a similar sense of humor. During my time with him, we would reminisce about our childhood in Lome and the things we used to do together. Our laughter during those conversations would especially get louder when some of the hilarious professors we had in middle school were mentioned.

One of them always came up. He was a professor of Ewe, our local language. Ewe was taught only in middle school and was an optional course. Many middle schoolers would take that course because the instructor, Mr. N, often came to class drunk and talked gibberish. As young as we were, we had a blast sharing jokes with him every time he came in impaired. Obviously, his mood was not consistent when he was drunk.

One minute he would look happy; the next minute he would threaten us of getting flogged for insubordination. All in all, he was still able to teach his course, but for the part, it was a class of laughter, relaxation, jabs, and punch lines between the students and Mr. N. If there is something today that still makes my conversations with cousin M. A. undeniably delightful, it would be our shared memories of Mr. N. Back then, these memories quelled my homesickness and the trepidation I constantly felt being in a foreign country and overwhelmed with the newness of everything.

As a foreigner in a strange land, I quickly realized that information was as rare and valuable as gold. My cousin was a very busy man with a full life. He was, at that time, juggling a full-time job with his classes at college. Still, he used every opportunity he had to discuss all his knowledge about job applications, getting his immigration paperwork in order, and getting acquainted with public transportation so that I would become familiar with the city and know the right places to go and find decent accommodation. Most importantly, he taught me about many socially acceptable and nonacceptable constructs. My cousin was a torchbearer of kindness—a trait I would learn to imitate as I became more acquainted with America over the years and stood on my feet. Years later, I played host to my cousin D. K. D. and his wife for a year when I lived in Hagerstown, Maryland, and then my brother K. A. A. when I lived in Knoxville, Tennessee. I would never have been able to play host if I didn't unconsciously have cousin M. A.'s guidance on what it means to be a meaningful host.

Even to date, my respect, admiration, and affection for my cousin M. A. remain undiluted. I was an immigrant with nothing but dreams in a strange land, and he took me in, shielded me, counseled me, and showed me incommensurable value. Many might believe it was because he was family, but I believe that is simply who he is. I have heard unbelievable stories about so-called family members who, in the glare of the harsh life abroad, become unrecognizable versions of themselves toward their kin, forgetting or just becoming indifferent to their roots. Many forget the African saying that the rooster that crows so proudly today must never forget that it was once an egg. Metaphorically speaking, my cousin is my egg; come what may, I will never forget this. Immigrants who discard the inherent value their egg has affected them are simply ingrates. There's just no nicer way to put it.

For me, America represents a lot of firsts. However, I doubt I can forget that it was the first place wherein my educated pride took a severe beating. Coming from a predominantly francophone country, I was at sea regarding English. I couldn't even understand it. This significantly affected me psychologically, battering my self-esteem, as the mocking around me from people I didn't even know got louder in my head.

In stores, my nervousness would cause me to speak gibberish, and I would be asked to repeat what I wanted as though I were a glorified moron. Finally, I decided that the language barrier I faced wouldn't turn me into a voiceless immigrant or make me feel less of an educated person despite my years of schooling in Togo.

There's a memory I have of being mocked repeatedly by one of my coworkers at the Target store. When I was attending graduate school in Raleigh, North Carolina, for a master's degree while also working a full-time overnight shift at the

Target store in Raleigh, there were times when one coworker in particular would mock my English. He was African American, heavily built, giant, and hardworking. He was a good employee except for one thing: he seemed to always think less of me. Other teammates working with him were lazy most of the time, but he was not. For that, I respected him. But often, when I went to him or a teammate near him for a question about our work or a brief conversation during our break, he would ask me to "speak English" and then stare at me with a big mocking smile.

At first I found it irritating. Then I decided to ignore it. I did not want to report him either because, to be fair, I was aware of the fact that my English was not great. Nevertheless, I decided to see in his mockeries nothing but stupid ignorance. His behavior also pushed me to renew my belief that whatever doesn't kill me is going to make me stronger. His negative energies toward me turned into positive energies channeled into my graduate studies. I gained renewed strength in studying my notes from class during my thirty-minute breaks at Target or going to class in the morning following my overnight shift. One day, however, I got fed up and confronted him.

As usual, he had uttered the same mockery, "Speak English."

I replied, "Do you know why I speak broken English?"

He laughed derisively but made no attempt to answer me.

"It is because while you were busy speaking English, which you cannot spell right, I was busy with my fluency in four languages. Remember that a man who speaks two languages is worth two men who speak only one," I stated boldly.

He stayed silent, watching me, because he was at a loss for words.

Emboldened by the silence, I proceeded to ask, "How many languages do you speak?"

He slowly put his two hands in his pockets, standing straight, and stared at me with no smile, silent. I politely walked away. We never had another conversation after that one. Then I left the overnight shift a few months after. That was because I graduated from my master's program and was moving to Tennessee for a PhD.

But even long before this scenario took place, I knew I had to become grounded in American English and become grounded fast. I have always been a problem-solver, so I looked around for a solution.

The English classes I wanted were outrageously costly, so I settled for a basic twice-a-week English course held in the public library at Gaithersburg, Maryland, by a gracious white woman. I got a job a couple of months later at KFC, working as a cook. I was relieved to be at the back of the restaurant, working quietly and limiting my interactions with the customers. The job became instrumental in fine-tuning my English through a slow but steady process. As I interacted better with coworkers and supervisors and followed instructions at my workplace, my conversational skills and confidence started to improve subtly.

The job was also helpful in my repayment plan for the loan my father had borrowed on my behalf. I found life in the States and life in Togo vastly different, almost of Grand Canyon proportions. Even though I had been well educated about American culture long before I came to America, the loneliness was jarring. Work predominated the lives of most people, as everyone was sucked into the perpetual dream-chasing that still characterizes the nation to date. The community-based warmth that nourished and watered my childhood was conspicuously absent, and during my early years, I missed it deeply.

America did fascinate me as a twenty-seven-year-old young black immigrant working hard to mold my destiny and struggling with English because I didn't want to be entangled in the insecurities that easily plagued me. I found America aggressively capitalist, shockingly individualistic, and admirably distinctive. I had read these things about America, but watching it all play out before my eyes was interesting. While there is much to learn, immigrants must be wary of embracing certain aspects of American culture. This is not a derogatory or condescending statement, but many of us must retain certain traces of our African roots, beliefs, stories, and ideologies. An environment can positively impact you, but it doesn't have to completely transform or alter who you have always wanted to be. Somehow the American atmosphere is so powerful and mentally influential that without an actively conscious mentality, a subtle alteration can take shape obliviously.

I do like the concept of the American dream. A dream that is age-old but thrives and soars irrespective of class, status, or background. A dream that is alive and available to all within America, as long as one is willing to grasp it with both hands and realize that it isn't free. I was one of those who clasped that dream. I like to believe it had been interwoven into my soul even before I stepped into American soil for the first time. It was also in America that I was tagged or deemed irrelevant due to my work and broken English. While America is a nation that can be kind, it is also one that often doesn't see beyond the surface of people. The racial construct is perhaps the most classic example of this. I didn't let that detract me from my path, nor did I let any perceived irrelevance diminish my self-worth. On the contrary, it made me stronger and more motivated to pivot higher and prove them all wrong.

One welcoming thing I found as an immigrant was the concept of punctuality. This fits well with my personality, as I cannot stand lateness. Tardiness drives me nuts ordinarily, and lateness has just never sat well with me. I have never understood it and don't want to understand it. I despise the popular saying about Africans and lateness. It is a stereotype, and I have avoided its projection upon me like the bubonic plague. The stereotype is a single subjective story. There are punctual Africans just like there are perpetual American latecomers.

As a society, America operates on well-defined schedules. This transcends corporate and business life into personal and community life. Coming from a well-connected and bonded community, the individualistic way of life was hard to adjust to for someone like me. It gives me mixed feelings. While it is almost relieving not to have family and friends show up unexpectedly at your doorstep or porch, extreme self-sufficiency places boundaries upon family, relationships, personal interference, and a sense of communal bonds. I wasn't sure how to feel about that. America is not a place where a community is invested in training a child.

After six months of holding a job at Kentucky Fried Chicken, I got a job at the Target store. My job there was physically strenuous, as I was expected to move, carry, stock, and climb the stairs with heavy merchandise as a backroom team member all night long. I invested in my job, even though I had lazy teammates who preferred to sleep or loiter around while a handful of us did the job. My sense of idealism or moral ethics wouldn't let me be a part of them. Laziness is only contagious when you let it be. Many of them snickered knowingly behind my back due to my supposed "stupidity" and how I loved working as an enslaved person. An *enslaved* person? The word made me laugh. I have never been one to turn myself away from hard work because, tell me, how else are you going to achieve what you need without hard work? Often I think the guys I worked with were more amused than spiteful.

"Why are you always all about the job?" I recall one of my lazy teammates asking one day.

"What do you mean?" I asked.

"You don't take breaks."

"We're given breaks," I countered.

"That's not what I mean, and you know it."

I shrugged in mock ignorance, unwilling to continue with the conversation. "We're paid to work."

He stared at me, eyes dancing with confusion, while I returned to carrying merchandise, pretending he didn't exist.

The snickering and "slave calls" didn't stop. Still, I was intelligent enough to understand that there is a world of difference between an enslaved person and an honest worker working diligently for his wages. I didn't have the luxury to be lazy anyway with loan repayment and responsibilities toward my family back home. I prioritized the repayment because it was of utmost importance that I did not let my father down by relinquishing my father's faith and trust in me. By spending money austerely, I was able to send something home monthly for monthly installment payments.

Beyond family, even though I had received student loans for my tuition fees, the job was instrumental in keeping me afloat during my years as a graduate student. It helped me to take care of daily expenses and pay for my apartment, books, and food. These needs were more important to me than baseless subjective, judgmental notions of character from people I barely knew or cared about.

My dedication to my meager job attained me the supervisor position within a year, and then I was admitted into the master's program at North Carolina. I kept my backroom store job in North Carolina, having been transferred to the Target store there. The job saw me through financially throughout my time at the university. The meager earnings afforded me no luxuries, but they did help. I had to use student loans to augment my meager income, but it is not a decision I regret because back then, my dreams were cherished, and I was willing to make necessary sacrifices to actualize them. To date, my student loans have not been paid off yet. I make minimum deposits every month, and I am in no rush for the process to be over. While I know my approach is not the best economic approach, I operate based on my belief of what works best for me. Those loans helped me to secure my future, and I'm glad they were available then.

Most people tend to experience a lot of culture shock when they move to a new environment. In my case, I wouldn't say it was distinctive, but it was manageable. I've talked about my language struggles and acceptance of certain parts of American civilization. Food also wasn't that much of a problem. I have always been a picky eater who eats in small portions. Back home, I shunned the national delicacies and favorites, so adjusting to food in the United States was easy. Food has never really been a priority for me. We all eat to stay alive, and we all need just a little every day to stay alive.

At this point, you must be wondering why I haven't touched on the subject of racism. After all, it is a deeply rooted and complex ideology that pervades the life of a black man in America. I encountered racism, and I will discuss my experiences in subsequent chapters. All in all, my migration to America is not something I will ever regret. America gave me a much better life and a journey filled with twists and turns.

I said at the beginning of this chapter that human beings are audacious. Our fearlessness stems from the fact that we are all built for adversity, even though many would rather run from it. Adversity is something I believe has plagued me in different ways, but like the mythical phoenix, I always rise from my ashes stronger and better than before. After all, the true test of a man is his ability to get back up stronger and far better than before.

Migration flung me out of my comfortable conventional world into a world where I made tremendous conscious progress, tasted success, and fully established a career. Migration taught me that sometimes in life, all you truly need is the courage to take that one bold step. Once you do, everything changes as long as you don't stop putting in the work. For me, that one bold step was leaving the shores of my beloved home country for another land to conquer the unknown.

I am grateful for that audacity.

Navigating life in a foreign country was a lot—overwhelming, daunting, complex, and oftentimes just downright strange and confusing.

Yet I persevered.

CHAPTER 4

Diving into Higher Education

R aleigh was a treasure trove of discoveries.
It was a melting pot and a turnaround too, the place where I began to ask myself introspective, unearthing, in-depth, and soul-searching questions. My thinking expanded, reaching monumental heights of inquiry. Raleigh was where I began to ask questions based on rational, skeptical, and unbiased evidence. It was the place where I officially stepped into the philosophical version of myself. It molded my mind into what it has become today. I moved to Raleigh, North Carolina, for my master's in French literature. Ironically, I had two management degrees from the University of Lome, so ordinarily, I didn't have any business diving into French literature.

Yet the deep-seated loneliness I had experienced in the last three years preceding my journey to Raleigh had unearthed something in me—the quest for philosophical inquiries about our existence. The intellectual gap and yearning I felt to have these questions answered could not be satiated by a graduate degree in finance, business, or management. My mind had evolved into much bigger dimensions. Money-making courses just wouldn't do. I desired more wisdom and more enlightenment to fill up the hunger that had been inadvertently born within my soul. Loneliness is brutal. It evoked and triggered a lot of unanswered questions in the darkest recesses of my mind. In my most private moments, reflections emerged and, with them, a box full of questions that had emanated from my unending gaze into my past.

What if I had not left my native country?

What if my life had not changed?

What if I still had my friends from my childhood memories? My neighborhood? And the schools I attended in Lome?

What if I had gotten a well-paying job in my home country?

What if I still attended the regular tick-the-box Sunday church service every week?

The mind can be a curious thing indeed. Blazing unapologetically into the future with uncertainty and optimism but somehow locked in the intersections of the past, it fascinated me.

I knew that my newfound passion for the humanities and social sciences would not be economically rewarding. But the mental thirst for philosophical knowledge was so great that I knew no amount of money was capable of quenching it. I had never been overly impressed or influenced by wealth. I didn't want to be well off economically but became enmeshed in strange insecurities, yearning deep within for answers I wasn't sure I would ever find. Besides, we don't say it often, but there is something wealthy about a beautiful mind and the vibrant enrichment it carries. It's indescribable, indecipherable, and unforgettable in many forms.

It might not sound reasonable to all, but studying literature brought a peace I had never known to the core of my existence. It was liberating and joyous in unexplainable ways. All my classes were intellectually stimulating and rewarding. No matter how stressful my nights had been at the Target store, I was always at class the following day. Often I'd fall asleep in class due to the stressful nature of my job, but I managed to always perform well. Academic failure or underperformance has never really resonated with me.

My routine at Raleigh was rigorous but well worth it. During those two crucial years, when I molded my future and did everything within my power not to underachieve in a new academic realm like French literature, my world quickly became a routine. I would spend my nights (ten to seven o'clock) working at the Target store. Then I'd drive home in the morning by eight o'clock, take a quick shower, and be on campus grounds at nine o'clock. I attended graduate classes between nine in the morning and two in the afternoon and studied in the library for one hour. I never missed this daily study habit—perusing course materials and checking out new books, drinking from a fountain of knowledge, and nourishing my mind.

My sleep hours were from four in the afternoon to nine at night, and I would be back at the Target store to begin my night shift at ten. My body adjusted to this five-hour sleep routine, and so like a built-in alarm clock, once it was nine o'clock, I would get up from bed and make it on time by ten o'clock. As a supervisor, I wasn't going to be caught dead getting there late. We were usually given two breaks during the night shift, a fifteen-minute and a thirty-minute break. I used the fifteen-minute break to eat and the thirty-minute break for my studies. I always brought my books to work, and most times, I would tackle my assignments there too.

Weekends and off days were tied up in reading and researching. French literature was demanding in terms of reading, writing, assimilating, and evaluating, but I enjoyed the intellectual rigor. I have come to appreciate the need for routine and systematic organization since then, and they still characterize my life to date. Nevertheless, I remained at the top academically. Until this point, I was firmly rooted in the belief that academic excellence had become intertwined into the tapestries of my existence. This was my presumption until I met a challenging course in my second year.

My professor, G. D., was intellectually intimidating. He had an impressive list of scholarly publications written in his name, and he taught literary theory with such finesse that every time class ended, I would be in awe of his beautiful mind. It was as though he had spent years seeking knowledge as a hidden treasure, found it, and his brains displayed all the gems he wore proudly.

As much as I admired Professor G. D., his course sometimes left me in a jitter. I studied it hard, harder than I studied other courses, yet it was as though I still had no chance of passing. A stellar presentation would make me pass the course with an excellent grade. Professor G. D. mandated us to present a chapter out of the 2,600 pages of *The Norton Anthology and Criticism Theory* textbook required for the course.

After much reflection, I ended up choosing a chapter on Walter Benjamin on the topic of the work of art in the age of mechanical reproduction. Having gained some knowledge of the appeal of video aesthetics and their effects, I channeled my video editing skills to create a stunning special effects explanation of my chapter on Walter Benjamin's theories and conceptual frameworks. My classmates were impressed, and my professor was delighted. The presentation boosted my grades and confidence in the course for the rest of the semester. Life, sometimes, is all about problem-solving.

French literature was a revelation. The knowledge accumulated through my readings and hours of study started to merge into a cohesive whole that ballooned into what would become a newfound philosophical mind. Several books are still memorable. As a sidenote, I'll always recommend books as the best knowledge providers. They are patient and quiet teachers capable of cultivating new worldviews and mind-altering discoveries. I spent time reading *La Condition Humaine* ("The Human Condition") by Andre Malraux and *Les Jeux sont faits* ("The Bets Have Been Placed") by Jean-Paul Satre. These books are like gemstones. The pages are steeped in legendary insights, all encased within graceful and artful writing. I was captivated. But it wasn't just books that opened my mind; it was the world around me.

I observed and understood the Westernized culture. As I read more, America's culture, mythological concepts, ideological constructs, and tribalism became clearer and more transparent. My new knowledge opened up the pathway for immense discoveries, but more importantly, a better-defined sense of Pan-Africanism emerged on a background of my open-mindedness. The longer I stayed in America, the easier it was to become acquainted with social, economic, and political constructs. I accepted them and lived with them, but my reflections on Africa and my homeland developed as I navigated better. I dug deeper into embracing my heritage and the intrinsically shaped values of my imperturbable African identity. My existentialism was formulated by one belief: the only race that truly matters is the human race.

Now, I am not writing about cultural or racial superiority. My views are completely subjective and come from a much deeper place. I was a full-grown adult when I developed my ideological constructs, and they have stayed with me ever since. I do not believe one race or cultural heritage is superior or better. I believe in true human connectedness. At the end of the day, the human race is one pulsating heart navigating the complexities of our world—some of which were created by our race. Learning how to adapt and navigate one culture while embracing another is a struggle most immigrants would relate to. In life, we all have to define ourselves so that others do not wrongly define us. This is even more critical when you live to dither between two worlds, so to speak.

My time in North Carolina was largely uneventful and steeped in routine. It passed quickly, and in two years, I graduated. My graduation day remains indelible in my mind simply because of my loneliness. At this time, I now had family in the States as opposed to when I first arrived. A bunch of immediate and extended family members and friends had also moved here in search of greener pastures. I extended invites to many of them, but none of them was able to attend. America had subdued them, entangling their lives in work and survival. I understood, yet I felt piercing loneliness in the depths of my soul, along with my fulfillment, pride, and elation. I have worked for this for two years. I had worked hard and smart, shuttling between a strenuous overnight full-time job and the demands of my studies. I had achieved it, yet I had no one to celebrate with.

There's something inherently powerful about that. Something unforgettable too. Along with loneliness, homesickness gnawed at me from within. Watching my classmates share the joy of the day with their families, loved ones, and well-wishers, I felt an indescribable stab of pain. I had no one to share my joy with. No one to pat me on the back and say, "Well done." No one to embrace, no one to take a picture with. On that day, I had no one. It's hard not to think about that day and not feel all the emotions run through my blood again. It was a bittersweet day.

In the end, I left earlier the graduation event than most others. I walked to my used car alone and drove off, whistling an off-key tune and keeping my face expressionless. When I saw my accumulated student loans, I was petrified. Yet nothing was going to stop me from the ultimate goal of my higher-education pursuits, not even frightful amounts of loans. It was time to apply for a doctoral program. Four months later, I was accepted into a doctoral program in Tennessee. My high GPA from North Carolina had secured me a scholarship, so I packed my bags and moved again.

I arrived in Knoxville on a windy Saturday filled with new dreams and hopes. I liked Knoxville immediately. Its beauty stunned me. It was a city that I knew would be kind to me. It bore no traces of the fearsome civil rights era I had read about. Instead, it was peaceful and explorative and surrounded by other remote towns. I rented a modest but lovely apartment near Henley Bridge. I would always have to cross it every morning as I went to campus, and as time went on, it became quite symbolic. I considered it the connector between my present and my future. It was a centerpiece that always made me remember not to give up on my dreams.

My doctoral program in Knoxville was supposed to run for four years: two years of coursework and two years to write and defend my doctoral dissertation. The first two years were a prerequisite to completing the courses, and as such, they were nonnegotiable. The last two years required a disciplined and independent schedule to produce a quality dissertation. Analyzing it all, I realized I could get it all done in three years instead of four. Now, this was not the usual protocol. This wasn't usually done, and for a while, I was unsure as to whether I could ask for it.

"Why not?" I asked myself one day. "What's the worst that could happen?"

A negative answer was the worst, so I was going to try and ask. The world doesn't work for closemouthed individuals.

And so, on a beautiful morning, I stood waiting outside my adviser's office to plead my case. I went over everything in my head, memorizing and memorizing what I had planned to say. I could do it; I could ask for this.

"Good morning, Kodjo!" my adviser greeted me cheerfully as he opened the door to his office. He was good-natured and naturally an optimist, one of those who could never truly be caught up or entangled in dark emotions.

I gave a tentative smile. "Good morning."

"I know you're always so punctual, but wouldn't you say you're a tad bit too early today?"

"I would like to discuss something with you," I explained.

"With me? Sure, come on in."

I stepped into the organized and well-maintained office.

"Please sit down."

I chuckled nervously. "This won't take long."

"Okay?"

"I'd like to know if it's possible to finish my doctoral program in three years instead of four," I blurted out.

My adviser's brows flickered up in surprise. He leaned back in his seat. "Well, this is a surprise," he said dryly. "You sure you are not going to take that chair?"

I sat down.

"Why?" he asked. "You just got to Knoxville, and it seems like you're plotting your way out already," he said with a humorous glint in his eye.

I chuckled again. "Just plotting an upward trajectory. I've analyzed everything, and I believe I can get it done in three years instead of four."

"Yeah?"

"Yeah," I said confidently.

He was watching me, waiting for more.

"The last two years are based upon my discipline and commitment. I don't need two whole years to deliver a quality dissertation. I have enough confidence in my academic abilities to know I can do it all in one year. I have everything to lose so that I won't jeopardize my future. A lot depends on it."

My adviser watched me while I held my breath.

"I must say that this is quite brave of you, Kodjo. I'm impressed. Your past academic records showed us that you are exceptional, so I have no real issues with your request, especially since you know it's all in your hands. Some protocols cannot be bypassed anyway, so you'll have to submit a written request to the doctoral committee, and if it's granted, you get to ride this thing for three years instead of four."

I smiled. "Thank you so much."

"I wish you all the best," he said.

I submitted my written request the following day to my doctoral committee, and based on my commitments and achievements within their program, my request was granted. I remember receiving the approval, savoring it, and becoming a true believer in my convictions all over again. Whatever I wanted, I could get. Whatever I strive for, I can achieve.

In between a tight study schedule, social life was nonexistent, but human relationships were not altogether absent. Many of my Tennessee friendships dissipated shortly after graduation, but one endured for a long time afterward. A wonderful, soulful, hardworking woman from Eastern Europe who dared to go back to school and chase her dreams of higher education became a good friend of mine. Her drive and tenacious attitude always struck me. It was infectious. It propelled mine to bigger heights. These days, life hasn't been kind to her, as she suffers from a few health complications, yet we are still in touch. I'm grateful for her educational achievements and how they continually provide her with a sense of worth for her time invested in schooling. Time is the most precious asset. It is always fulfilling to know you spent it well in the past. Although she moved to South Carolina with her husband, I still take time to keep in touch and nurture our friendship.

Two faculty professors stand out in my mind as nurturers, mentors, and guiding lights. As a native speaker of French with excellent command of its structure, coupled with my extensive class participation, my two French faculty professors found it easy to talk to me and cultivate an easy relationship with me.

Back in Togo, respecting and fearing our professors came naturally, and we did it flawlessly. America doesn't demand that, but I still retained that idea of respecting those ahead of me. Those who know more than you and have walked the path before you. I never feared them, but I respected them and was always scrupulously polite and proper while speaking. This endeared my professors to me.

One of them, Professor E. C., still sends me handwritten letters to date, twelve years after I had graduated. His mentorship and trust were invaluable. I still send him handwritten holiday cards every year as well. Professor E. C. was not a black immigrant, but he touched my life with his humanism and the way he took a keen interest in me. He talked to and advised me as a father, and his unforgettable contributions to my life went beyond academia. He was warm toward the African in me without denying his race or origin. He constantly tried to prove to his colleagues that even though I was African, he understood me better. This didn't, of course, go down well with all of them. They all valued me as their student and wished me success, but only Professor E. C. somehow felt responsible for my success.

Professor E. C. was eventually forced into retirement. His peers frequently complained that he was no longer productive enough to remain a professor. At that time, his early symptoms of Alzheimer's had started to show. He found himself repeating his materials in several classes. This coincided with the time he criticized his peers for treating him unfairly. He was a blunt man, always giving his mind every time. In one isolated incident, he openly criticized his colleagues in my doctoral committee to their faces about their inability to grasp the intricacies of African literature, which was my research topic. Of course, this did not sit well with them. Like most other spheres, the academic world can often be steeped in the contest of ego. I usually do not blame them because, well, if I'm being honest, it takes a lot to be renowned in the academic world. Being bestowed with the title of professor comes with years of hard work and grit. So when one questions your intellect, it can feel like a blow. The doctoral committee members were not willing to simply just take a blow without striking back, and they were willing to use me to do it.

"Step in here for a quick chat, Kodjo," one of the members said to me one morning, pretty early and before anyone else arrived.

"Good morning," I said with a smile.

The salt-and-pepper-haired professor smiled back but avoided my eyes, knowing the gravity of what he wanted to say.

"I'll get straight to the point, Kodjo. We need you to remove Professor E. C. as a member of your doctoral committee so that the other committee members can stay. But of course, you know they are not willing to keep working with him, right?"

I kept my face neutral and almost expressionless. "Yeah."

"I understand you have an admirable closeness with him and that he's your mentor, but I'm sure you wouldn't want that familiarity to get in the way of your degree, would you?"

I was silent for a long time. "No, I wouldn't," I responded.

The professor nodded. "Very good, you know what to do."

I had instantly recognized but disliked the subtle manipulation. All my committee members were valuable to me, and I didn't like having to choose. Yet it had become a necessary imperative. I explained everything to Professor E. C. as best as I could, and thankfully, he did not take it personally. He saw instead the bigger picture and the most important thing— finishing up. This was all the motivation he needed to support me till the end. Professor E. C. is still alive to date. I'm glad I still get to be a part of his life.

Another professor who impacted my life and became a friend was Professor J. R. I took a few of his courses during the first two years of my doctoral studies, and we developed a strong intellectual bond. It's hard not to picture him now without the freckled face, the million-dollar smile, the insane sense of humor, and his brilliant scholarly mind. Our friendship grew when he selected me to be a part of his summer study abroad program in France as his teaching assistant. This was at the end of my first year in their graduate program, and then I accompanied him again in my second year.

Those two summers were fun and adventurous even though they were purposefully for academic pursuits. We taught undergrad students and then traveled through the gorgeous city of Paris, drinking in beautiful sights and checking out the Loire Valley of France. It was a real experience for me. One that I truly cherished and one that I emulated when, two years later, I created my own study abroad program in the nation of Senegal. To date, Professor J. R. and I still enjoy each other's company and have mutual respect. Often we amuse ourselves by sharing friendly jokes about serious topics like the existentialist philosophy of extraordinary scholars like Jean-Paul Sartre.

My graduation from Tennessee was my proudest moment as an immigrant. For the first time since I had gotten on that plane in Lome, where my family had come to wish me well, I truly felt that my struggles were over. The graduation ceremony was held months apart from my American citizenship allegiance ceremony. This time around, I desperately wanted my family here with me to celebrate my success. My older brother B.

K. A. agreed to come to the United States to represent my family. I was excited. With enthusiasm pumping through my blood, I requested an official invitation letter from my university that would be instrumental in granting my brother a visitor visa from the United States Embassy in Togo. The letter was given, but when my brother took it over there, he was denied the visa under the claim that they were unsure he would return to Togo.

To explain how ludicrous this sounded, the US Embassy denied a visitor's visa to a grown man who simply wanted to attend his brother's doctoral graduation. A grown man with a wife and kids, a thriving medical career as a surgeon, a full-time academic position at Togo's medical school, and who was co-owner of a clinic. The US Embassy, for some reason, had some conviction that this man would abandon the life he had built for himself and his family and become an illegal immigrant in the United States if he was given a six-month visa to attend his brother's graduation.

It's one thing to feel loneliness. It's different to have it thrown in your face by powers that dominate things you have no control over. I was beyond devastated. More so, I had to control the rage thrumming within me because of the reckless way power had been displayed. Once again, I was going to graduate alone. I would have no one to embrace me, say "Well done," and take memorable pictures with. Inwardly, I seethed at America. I seethed so badly that I thought fleetingly about tearing apart my newly acquired citizenship. Yet I knew I wouldn't do it because I had worked too hard to just toss it aside. Tearing it apart in a moment of pain and disappointment meant I would disregard my hard work all these years. After all, citizenship was, in essence, a side effect of my goal of having a higher education.

I put my pain aside and went to my graduation stage that day to become officially bestowed with the doctor of philosophy in literature title. Years of research studies, reading hours, brainstorming sessions, exams, and endless analytical thinking had all culminated at this moment. After that, I watched friends, families, and well-wishers hug and cheer for their loved ones who got the same terminal degree I had. The loneliness started seeping deeply into me again, choking and stirring. I had once again extended invites to most family and friends in the United States, but none was capable of attending. Their lives were still entangled in work. Amid my crushing isolation among the crowd, I saw cousin M. A. and his wife and two kids from Maryland. It was a pleasant surprise because he had not assured me he would make it. I don't think I can ever forget his eyes watering with warmth and delight as he hugged me and said, "I'm proud of you."

Most days in our lives are characterized by nothingness and bland routine. But then there are those other days filled with gems that are so unforgettable because of the grandeur of depth and beauty that leave one speechless. My graduation day was one of those days. I never forgot the love and swift evaporation of the alienation I was feeling, thanks to cousin M. A.

A few months later, I was hired as a university professor in Upstate New York. A voiceless immigrant who once had nothing but aspirations and hopes was now boldly living the American dream.

CHAPTER **5**

Death, Grief, and Adversity

I have always believed that the elements that characterize death are somewhat fascinating.

I once read somewhere that the death of a loved one was a curious thing. We all know that our time in this world is limited and that, eventually, we will end up under the sheets or six feet underground, never to wake up. And yet it is always a surprise whenever it happens to someone we know. Death is like walking up to your room upstairs in the dark and thinking erroneously that there is one more step than there is. Then your foot falls through the air, and there is a sickly moment of dark surprise as you try and readjust the way you think of things.

Death is powerful, unstoppable, unpredictable, and yet fathomable. The countdown to our deaths begins the day we are born. And then, when it happens, we float back into the eternal sphere from which we all emanated. Death breeds fear in human beings, and I cannot blame anyone who fears death. It is natural for humans to fear what they do not know and what they cannot control. Yet we often forget that, like Mark Twain once stated, we were dead for billions of years before birth and never suffered the slightest inconvenience. Life is fragile and short. Living is sweet, yet life is a beautiful lie, and death is a harsh, grim reality. An inevitable reality.

Grief is born out of love and loss. The harder you grieve, the deeper it shows how much your heart misses a person. I learned that grief is incredibly devastating. Therefore, it is important to create and develop important coping mechanisms.

Personally, that mechanism lies in my mind within the depths of my thought processes. I believe deeply in my mental strength. Therapy during grief isn't something that would work for me because it would leave me feeling vulnerable. The feeling of vulnerability for me is counterproductive for my brain to bounce back from hardship, pain, and sorrow. Self-therapy has always been an efficient solution for me. Finding my inner peace and reconnecting with my profound beliefs, like the conviction that what doesn't kill me will make me stronger. Grief occurs in different ways for all of us. Studying the psychology-based models for the distinctive stages of grief, I accepted that it wasn't uniquely tailored to my mind, personality, and ideology, even though it helps a lot of people get back on their feet. What is popularly referred to as the healing stage is something I have learned to consciously reject for myself when I cope with grief.

I do not want to learn how to heal after an unfortunate situation has caused me to grieve. I stay connected with painful reminiscences to keep me connected with my reality and step seamlessly into everyday life while moving on. It would surprise you to know that this does not keep me miserable. On the contrary, I feel blessed to receive enriching energies from my joys and sorrows. Death breeds grief, and both give birth to emotional adversity. Every human, at some point in their life, will have no choice but to confront both. As for me, I have been plagued by both in distinctive ways. Humans are a product of their experiences, so it's easy to say that my experience with grief has molded me to a large extent.

Three different experiences stand out the most in my mind.

- **Jacob**

Whenever I remember my friend Jacob, I'm reminded of the fact that he was a heavenly angel wrapped up in human flesh. He was admirably unique and special. Even in death, no one has managed to win against the effect he had on me in his lifetime. Jacob and I were age-mates who had grown up in Kodjoviakope. I met Jacob during a vulnerable period in my life. At the time I met him, I was looking for ways to be free from the bullying and intimidation that plagued my life. Growing up, I was always small and skinny, brains notwithstanding. The older boys in class, seeing as they were not as bright as I was, subjected me to immense bullying. They would forcefully try to grab my food, and if I dared to resist or stand up to them, I would be slapped around. On other days, they would rain verbal abuse on me to diminish my self-esteem. This became a repetitive pattern in my life until it transformed into normalcy. I got used to it, happy and content to just be home safe day after day. Bullying is more ingrained in the daily life of African schools, and it hardly ever makes the news—neither is it deemed as overly important or crucial. If you're being bullied, you either learn to take care of yourself or stand up for yourself.

On a languorous Sunday afternoon, I watched a karate movie. My young mind was mesmerized by the skinny Asian martial artist beating up his adversaries who were so much bigger than him. I was fascinated. Up until then, I had never seen or heard of anything like it. I consciously compared the bloodied and beaten bandits to the bullies in my school who never let me be. As the days coalesced into weeks, I increasingly ruminated over the movie. The bullying did not stop, and whenever the bullies came for me, I would imagine myself like the hero martial artist beating them to a pulp in such a way that they would never dare to come ten meters close to me. The movie became a revelation. I realized that I wanted to be like a martial artist. I, too, wanted to have the skill of defense. Even though I had come to manage and accept bullying as a part of my life, somehow I understood that I wanted it to end. I decided to join a karate club. The conviction became absolute and solidified within me; I was sure that I would not rest until I found a karate club that would accept me.

In no time, my obsession led me to find a club, and that was when I met Jacob, the instructor. He was slightly intimidating at first, so I concentrated more on karate than on building up a friendship with him. I became better and better, and my developing skills led to fluid banter and, subsequently, a friendship that would propel me to instructor assistant after I attained a black belt six years later. My reputation as a black belt was enough to bring bullying to a screeching, grinding halt in my life. I never even had to use my skills on anyone, except at the many tournaments and competitions where fatal injuries and lifesaving regulations applied. Although I know, I wouldn't have hesitated to use them if the need had ever arisen.

One memorable day stands out in my mind. I was only two years into my karate study, an orange belt at the time. Jacob and I had somewhere to go after my school hours, and he had come to get me. On our way out of the school gates, we encountered my bullies. Ordinarily, whenever I saw them, my heart would constrict in my chest, and I would avoid their eyes and their path. But not on that day, I had my karate skills, and they boosted my confidence, and my bullies knew that. If I were alone, I would have silently passed by them. But having regaled Jacob with stories about them, Jacob being Jacob, he couldn't pass up the opportunity to have some fun.

"Hey, Ray!" he called out loud enough for them to hear. Jacob always called me Ray. "Aren't those the losers who used to snatch your food?"

I smiled. The things my friend could say with a straight face. "Yeah!" I responded enthusiastically.

The boys turned around, eyes spewing hostility and suppressed rage.

"Ooh, what a frown! Stop tightening those muscles!" Jacob said, smiling and enjoying himself.

One of the boys came closer, walking threateningly toward us. I was instantly at Jacob's side. There were four of them, and he and I could easily take them. I didn't want a fight to break out though; school rules were still school rules, and I was still an academic star.

"What's the problem?" I asked the boy.

"He's pissed because there's no food to snatch today," Jacob offered, and we both giggled.

The muscles in the boy's face tightened.

"Walk away," Jacob ordered. From the tone of his voice, it wasn't a suggestion.

"You wouldn't want to take on an upset black belt, now, would you?" I asked with irony.

Jacob and I stood waiting and watching. The boy's friends and fellow bullies stood from afar, watching.

"You'll regret this," he said angrily before ambling back to his friends.

"Yeah right," I said. Regret what exactly? I never did regret anything, and it had felt good to stand up to them for once.

My friendship with Jacob blossomed as we spent time with each other, discussing the club's future, partaking in karate competitions, and becoming each other's confidants. We learned about our respective strengths, doubts, weaknesses, and secrets. Even when I moved to the United States, time and distance did not shirk or botch our friendship. Our connection and camaraderie did not fall into the cracks of space and time even though we were oceans apart.

Whenever I returned to Togo to visit, I always made it a priority to surprise him with a visit. We would eat local food, go out on the town, and immerse ourselves in recollections. I learned so much from Jacob: the nobility of gratitude, the power embedded in martial arts, the value of humility, and most importantly, the beauty embedded in true friendship. He put me on the pathway to a discovery of my inner voice. I learned the art of "show, don't tell" from him. He taught me about my inherent metaphysical dimension that only my meditative growth was allowed to experience and nurture. Jacob was one of a kind. Our friendship was one of a kind. I loved him. In essence, he became my brother.

Seven years ago, precisely in the spring of 2015, Jacob passed away from a heart condition. It had been too sudden. It was as though we received the prognosis and he died suddenly before there was even time to begin to process some level of hope. His death shook me to the core of my soul. I was wracked with bitter disbelief and torn up by grief. His passing left a large, gaping void in my heart that I was unable to share with anyone. Our memories and friendship remain sacred to me up until this day. I hardly ever talk about him to just anyone. Our hearts all have boundless depths, and there is so much hidden within them. A man is never truly dead as long as he stays alive in the heart of another. Jacob lives on in my heart. He was all shades of inspiring and unforgettable and, by all means, irreplaceable.

I miss you, my brother. They say only the good die young. I guess that will forever remain one of life's most unending mysteries.

Until I see you again.

- **Clement**

I met Clement in high school. While I wouldn't call him my best friend, he was one of my buddies. From high school, we attended the only university in Lome and graduated together with a master's degree in management. We were good friends then, hanging out with other members of our social circle, but while we were in Togo, he never really stood out from my other friends.

Two years after graduation, I was on a plane to the United States to shape my destiny, and I never heard from him again. Eleven years later, Clement surprisingly sauntered into my life when we coincidentally met in Senegal. I was leading a study abroad trip from my university in New York. Clement had settled in Senegal and had become a thriving business owner in the country. We were delighted to see each other. They say the world is small, but until that moment when I met Clement and we laughed, talked endlessly, and reminisced about our time in school, I had not experienced the littleness of the world. My study trip to Senegal was primarily dominated by my students and what we had gone there to do, but the unprecedented nature of Clement's presence sprinkled the trip with additional flavor.

Whenever we were not too busy, we would spend time exploring the city of Senegal. Clement knew the most interesting places, and he was an awesome conversationalist. He was handsome too, with his well-trimmed tiny beard and intelligent dark-brown eyes that missed nothing. We talked about our lives and his businesses, and he regaled me with stories about his successes and pitfalls.

Despite everything, he was striving, thriving, and soaring, and it delighted my heart to see him successful and prosperous. To me, Clement defined the notion of "Life is what you make of it." Just like some of us, he had decided to leave our homeland to seek out more opportunities, and he had done so well for himself. He had hoisted himself up from the dregs to a respectable place in life. I was proud of him. I celebrated with him. I have always been one to cheer on the wins and varying successes of friends. It is always refreshing to see those who define what accomplishment should look like for themselves and then go on to achieve it.

Every summer since we first bumped into each other ten years ago, whenever I took my students on the annual study abroad trip, I would seek Clement out and we would have a wonderful time together. In those quality hours we spent together, Clement metamorphosed into a good friend and then a best friend. We became each other's confidants. I started to trust him more and more. I trusted him better than those who had become my good friends in the States. He possessed an innate and highly remarkable business intelligence. His mind was always brimming with superb business ideas that he would enthusiastically share with me. For Clement, it did not matter how much he had achieved. There was always more to achieve. He ceaselessly invited me to become an investor in one of his numerous businesses that yielded enormous financial returns, but I've just never been one to be carried away or lured by the promise of money. I was always charmed to see him win and thrive, stepping in from one sphere of business success to another.

A year and a half ago, while I was in Dakar, Clement suggested visiting me in the States, and I happily obliged. I was thrilled. We decided to prepare for his trip during the summer period. My mind was awash with plans for all the fun activities we would have together. I carefully selected the places I would take him to visit and the things and people I would introduce to him. After all this time, he would be stepping into my world, and I was going to make sure that I would at least match the level of hospitality and generosity he had always shown me, if I could not surpass it. We made plans to leave for New York City together and booked the same flight departing from Dakar. A week before our departure, Clement told me he wasn't feeling too well and had come down with a slight fever. We made jokes about it, believing it to be so trivial and insignificant that he would be back on his feet in no time. The following day I traveled out of town and returned in the evening. I placed a phone call to Clement, and he answered me cheerfully. He sounded better, as though he was blazing his way toward a path of full recovery. I joked with him about his long work hours as a CEO and how he needed a break. I visited him that night, and we had dinner over our fluid and easy banter. As the night wore on, I had to leave to write some reports for my academic research. He also needed to rest for our upcoming trip, so we said our goodbyes, promising to speak the following day.

At 11:00 a.m. the following day, I received a phone call, one that I have been unable to forget ever since.

"Hello?"

"Mr. Adabra?" the female voice on the other line tried to confirm.

"Yeah," I responded. "Who is this?"

"I'm an employee of your friend, Mr. Clement. I'm calling to inform you he just died." Her voice trembled from hoarseness, and it was easy to note that she had been crying.

I clutched the phone hard, unable to formulate the right words, as I sat down in disbelief. It was as though she had just dumped a bucket of ice-cold water on me.

What was I hearing? Clement was dead? Clement was dead! How? When? Why?

"Mr. Adabra, are you there?" the female voice asked me.

"I . . . yeah, I . . . I'm here."

The rest of the conversation was immersed in interrogation. My confusion and pain were glaring, and so was hers. Somehow death had ambled toward my friend and abruptly terminated his journey in this world just five days before our forthcoming trip that we had been looking forward to. The fickleness and unpredictability of life were apparent to me, and it felt ugly and tasted bitter.

Death, where is thy sting?

The following day I was confronted with the grotesque reality of Clement's sudden death as I stood and watched his dead body lying at the morgue. The same body that had been thrilled with life and vitality just last night when we had dinner. How could he just die like that? How? There was no answer, and there would never be.

On the day of our scheduled flight, I sat beside an empty seat—the place where Clement would have sat as he displayed his usual effervescence and vibrancy. It was hard to stop thinking about how different the flight would have been if he had been there with me. I was so upset that I began to silently tear up, ignoring the movie I could have watched. When I landed in New York, it was hard not to think about how different New York City would have felt if he had been by my side. I imagined the things he would have said, what he would have observed, what he would like about the city, and what he wouldn't. The pain was intense. It was as though I was carrying a ton of bricks that was too heavy for my heart. Grief permeated my soul. Questions wracked my mind as I tried to make sense of and find meaning from this sudden and excruciating loss.

After I landed at JFK, I took a domestic flight to my town, still encased in my pain and grief. On the outside, I appeared normal, but internally, I was shattered. Another gaping hole had just become a void, and I was wondering how I was supposed to live with yet another void. I called Uber, arrived home, and noticed my house steeped in unusual darkness. Believing my wife was asleep, I quietly got out my keys, opened the door, and entered the house. Shutting the door as quietly as I could, I went upstairs. Even while I was on the stairs, the emptiness started to hit me. My wife had shockingly moved out her things while I was away on my trip. I searched the rooms, the kitchen, and the basement, calling out her name in panic.

Empty silence. She was gone for good, never to return.

I sat down in silence, stunned and reeling at the same time from two important people leaving my life four days apart. I wondered why fate had decided that it was okay to hit me with two vicious twists in such a short period. At that moment, I couldn't properly process how I was feeling. Shock was the most dominant emotion, while pain and despair struggled within me for more dominance. Life, at that moment, felt like a cruel joke.

The summer of 2021 had turned gloomy.

• **The Divorce**

I met my ex-wife when I was a sophomore student in Togo, bristling with my dreams and ambitions, believing that my intelligence and sound mind would effectively propel me to a better place. I rolled with my peers, invested myself in my studies, and prided myself on making it through an educational system orchestrated with ineptitude. I met my ex-wife on one of those languorous days when I chilled with my friends at our usual corn porridge-and-donut shop. Is it ironic that I met her the same exact way I met my first girlfriend? And at the same location? As I have said before, most days in our lives are characterized by routine and sameness, but there are always those days that are coated with rarity and are all shades of unforgettable. Those days when an alteration happens in your world as you know it. That alteration can come in different forms. It could be in the form of an opportunity, a revelation of an epiphany, or a person.

On this languorous evening after our usual study sessions, a year after my first relationship had ended, I was with my three friends at the corn porridge shop. We were our usual selves, effervescent and fun, pervading the entire atmosphere with our teasing, laughter, and conversations. Out of nowhere, my eye caught a beautiful young woman walking down the street at a fast pace. Her walk was focused and determined, and it was evident that she was undisturbed by the evening activities unfolding around her and was only interested in getting to her destination. She wasn't smiling, but her soul was. She was not interested in the attention she was arousing from anyone, and she barely said a word to anyone until my friend T. A. A. called out to her. Is it ironic, too, that he knew her just like he knew my ex-girlfriend?

She turned to him with a mesmerizing and surprised smile. They engaged in little desultory talk, and then he wished her a good evening. She briefly turned to Brother R, A. F., and me, greeted us with a smile, and promptly left. T. A. A. was a classic ladies' man with a well-established reputation in our neighborhood. The minute she left, I asked him questions about her. Who was she? What was her name? How did he know her? Was he interested in her? Was he involved with her? Had he had any amorous adventure with the angelic young woman?

T. A. A. was amused by my interest, but he answered my questions. He was not interested in her, he had no amorous relationship with her, and her name was Ms. J. He could indirectly facilitate an introduction if I wished, and I eagerly accepted. T. A. A.'s girlfriend at the time was friends with Ms. J. She was assigned the task of bringing me into Ms. J.'s world. On a sunny afternoon, she convinced Ms. J. to accompany her to the house of her boyfriend's friend, to whom she had to deliver a message.

So three weeks after I had first laid my eyes on her, Ms. J., in the company of her friend, came to my house. She didn't remember me from that evening, but I managed to get her interested in the delightful conversation that T. A. A.'s girlfriend and I had managed to plan for the evening. The conversation flowed, and the vibe felt right between us. Subsequently, we met again in the following weeks, and when my mother first met her, she liked her and told me she was "wife material." Within a few weeks, we had become a couple.

Unlike me, who had grown up and developed within the warmth and love of a close-knit nuclear family, my future wife had not been so lucky. She did not have a family that was truly interested in her growth. They did not send her beyond elementary school, and at the time I met her, she was in a trade school learning how to become a tailor.

Three years into our relationship, I left for the United States. Before I left, her family members had mocked her, telling her she was deceiving herself if she was convinced that an educated guy like me from a middle-class family would be serious about marrying her, especially since I was leaving the shores of Togo. The condescension broke my heart. I promised not to disappoint her, to marry her, and to prove to her that her family members were wrong about us. Most importantly, I loved her and was dedicated to proving that to her no matter what. Our long-distance relationship lasted for eight years. During those years, she moved out of her family home and stayed with my parents. We stayed united, prayed for better days, and weathered storms together.

I married her two years after my departure when I first visited. It was important to me to be a principled man and keep my promise. It was also important to me that our marriage thrived and worked despite the time and distance that separated us. Six years later, American Immigration Services approved our application so she could join me.

At the time she joined me in the United States, I had a staggering amount of student loans accumulated from my years in the graduate programs I completed. I was still dedicated to giving her a good life and facing whatever financial upheavals we had. I did my best to provide for her and to always have our finances in order. For a woman who had stayed in Africa all her life and then was suddenly in the United States, the challenges were a lot, but we got through them together. She learned English as a second language in adult class so she could work. She learned how to drive, got her first car, and then her first job as a housekeeper in a senior living community. She made more friends and even passed her citizenship test. I was proud of her on that particular milestone because I knew how hard she had studied for it.

Our marriage was not perfect. We had our ups and downs. Perhaps the biggest problem we had to face was the ideological conversion that had taken place between us. As time went on, and as we stayed far away from home, the divergence in our views of African heritage and identity began to widen. Slowly my ex-wife began to disconnect from the urge to physically go back to our roots and keep the strong ties we had with the African continent, and this was critical to me. I was not against her embracing our new environment, but we needed to remain unshakable in our roots. What was a core value to me had become of little importance to her, and it deeply saddened me. This began to underlie every other issue we had. It began to quietly fire the fan of conflicts we had. Subsequently, our intimate life witnessed a decline.

Two years ago, just a few months before my summer trip to Senegal, the one that Clement was supposed to accompany me back on, my ex-wife started to entertain the idea of separation. She informed me that she was no longer happy with our marriage and she wanted out. My Togolese roots had never prepared me for divorce. I grew up watching my parents stick together no matter what. I had always believed that in a marriage, both parties could weather any storm the way I had grown up seeing my parents do. So it wasn't a surprise when it was me who requested we seek marital counseling. Divorce was not an acceptable option because it felt as though I was breaking the promise I had made long ago to marry her. In our last conversation, before I left for Dakar to bring Clement with me, I revisited the counseling option so we could try to save what we had.

"You're still down for it?" I asked for clarifying purposes.

She hesitated. "I told you before, I don't think it's going to work."

"No harm in trying," I said, giving her a wan smile.

"Let's talk about it when you return from your trip," she suggested.

Since Clement was going to come back with me, maybe we could have fun together and we would be reminded of the sweetness of the old times. I returned to an empty home with the heavy weight of Clement's unexplainable death weighing heavily on me. She was gone, and she wanted to stay gone because she firmly insisted on no therapy sessions but the divorce when I reached out to her. Whenever I recalled myself saying, "No harm in trying," I was overwhelmed by an angry sense of betrayal.

Yet I promised myself I would honor her decision. She had the right to choose her happiness, and since it could not be found within the confines of our marriage, then so be it. A year ago, our divorce was finalized. The end of it all plummeted me into an abyss of depression and then more depression. For seven months, I was floating within depths of sadness and waves of despair and grief, with work as my only anodyne. The brutality of loneliness descended upon me again, searing and deep. It was as though it knew me by name by now. The thing about loneliness is that it sweeps right through, and it will never be ignored. Unlike what I had felt during the years I graduated, it felt worse. It felt eternal this time around, plummeting me into the dark unknown. And at first, I feared I couldn't escape.

They say time heals all wounds. I say that time only makes it easier to cope as we go on in life. Emotional injuries are just as scorching and as burning as physical ones. It's like having a nasty injury on a leg and getting treated but being left with a limp and scars. Regardless, you learn to live with the limp—to walk with it, jump with it, and even dance with it. I learned to be okay with being by myself. I wasn't particularly impressed with the usual conventional consolations I got.

"Oh, don't worry, all will be well."

"You'll be fine."

That was the best that anyone could say. Would it be fine? Nothing was fine.

On a day that wasn't filled with any special significance, I realized that I was stronger than the pain. No one was coming to save me, so it was time to become my hero. Everyone can be their hero, and I was angry with myself that I had ignored mine for so long. I reached out to it, pulled it toward me, and let it strengthen me. I started to smile again, leave my bed in the morning, go to the movie theater by myself, go for long strolls on Ontario beach by myself, do my cooking, and delve into the soulful music that pervaded the '80s and '90s. The tears stopped as I became much more comfortable with my new but unusual life.

To date, my self-care routines have not changed. I take myself to the movies every week to enjoy a good movie. I still take myself to the beach to enjoy the refreshing breeze of the ocean. New York is blessed with beautiful parks, so I take myself to some of them regularly. I've always been a lover and fervent admirer of nature. Physical conditioning, workouts, martial arts, and mental meditation are all elements I retain in my life as part of my self-love rituals. Intellectually, I continue to invest in my scholarly endeavors and enhance the learning process of my students.

- **My Discoveries**

The deaths of Jacob and Clement, two of my closest friends in the world, taught me that no matter how much I raged at life, I had to find a way to learn how to smile back at life once again, even when life battered me with struggles and challenges. Their deaths made me accept the fickleness of this world and taught me better about the inescapable fate of all humans—death.

Death plays an elusive hide-and-seek game until it boldly steps out of the shadows to claim our souls. I found inspiration in what the Roman emperor and stoic philosopher Marcus Aurelius once said: "Death smiles at us all. All a man can do is smile back." Remember that blockbuster Roman Empire movie *Gladiator* released back in the year 2000? This was one of its most classic and memorable lines.

I missed Jacob and Clement profoundly. To handle my grief, I traveled to remote locations, but my all-time favorite remains the peaceful, calming, and soothing ocean. It has a way of awakening my inner peace trapped within my soul, a symbolic journey that allows me to cross through visually invisible, multidimensional doors into a mental space that defeats all my worries, doubts, fears, anxieties, disappointments, and fatigue birthed from unforeseeable life events and human folly. During those draining periods of mental, physical, and emotional hardship, that form of self-therapy best defines my approach to overcoming the difficulties that cross my life's path. It has always mattered to me that I unapologetically revive my self-therapeutic way of reclaiming my peace and the essence of my existence.

Everyone has a way of dealing with grief, pain, adversity, and loss. Humans are defined by their intrinsic differences. *Different*, in this context, is inherently beautiful and powerful. It is significant too, because unless we learn to rise above adversity, we are submerged in waters of hurt and pain. In truth, I have faced surreal and baffling hardships in life. Nevertheless, especially through the death of two of my best friends, I learned to awaken an energy element. My energy sprouts wings that allow me to fly to the skies, propelling me to a place in the clouds where I can place my misfortunes to be swallowed by destiny. This does not mean that when I fly back down, I simply just forget. I only assuage the old pain within my memories and transform it into motivational energy that strengthens me. The painful recollections do not weigh me down with sadness but push me to bigger heights. After all, a wise old African man once said, "It is at the end of the old rope that we weave the new."

And so, while my pain is channeled to something better, I meditate, redefine my priorities, and smile back at life. I firmly believe that what doesn't kill you makes you stronger. It might sound cliché, but it carries a weighty truth: Humans are equipped to survive, grow beyond adversity and loss, and come out stronger from it. I have strong faith in my internal voice, just the way religious people have faith in God. Achieving mental vitality comes from the development of mental convictions and doing everything to bring those convictions to fruition. As long as we are on this voyage we all are blessed to call life, it will always have one or two pivotal lessons to teach us if we can only just listen and pay attention. Life is like a class. I always strive not to fail at it. Who assigns us our grades? The answer to this question is wrapped up in multifaceted tapestries, so I wouldn't attempt to answer it. Only arrogant humans can claim to be purveyors of eternal truths.

Since I have learned to prioritize self-love, I've learned that making my happiness important is my responsibility. While I was a married man, I had gotten accustomed to not prioritizing my happiness. The marriage vow we had repeated were the same conventional marital vows reiterated around the world:

To have and to hold from this day forward, for better, for worse, for richer and for poorer, in sickness and in health, to love and to cherish until death does us part, this is my solemn vow.

I know I am not speaking from a subjective view when I say this. During happy times, it's easy to keep a vow. No one complains when things are gliding all smoothly. However, when things go south—and this is common within the Western space—one partner is always quick to prematurely ask for a divorce based on "unhappiness" or "irreconcilable differences." It's justifiable to ask what happened to those vows that were so easy to adhere to when happiness was the norm.

I wrote in the first chapter that my parents remained married to date, even though they weren't the exact definition of a perfect couple. Despite major issues cropping up between them as I grew up, they stayed loyal to their vows, and as such, they stayed loyal to each other, and their marriage continues to thrive. This is an unpleasant truth that most people do not want to hear: If you want to stay married forever, you have to shut the divorce door and put in the work. The mindset has to be one of "us against the world." My parents' marriage was an inspiration to me. I wished to mold my own marriage after theirs, to pattern it after what they had taught me, even though I was well educated about the alarming rate of divorces in the Western world.

However, I had to realize and accept that I wasn't married to a person with the same conditioning. Africans, by nature, aren't fans of divorce. So when mutual friends tried to convince my ex-wife to stay so that we could resolve our differences, she gave them a three-word timeless response:

"This is America."

I had smiled bitterly at that. Yeah, sure, this was America, the land that exalted and extolled the concept of self-happiness no matter what. The land of a 50 percent divorce rate. The land that glamorizes the concept of the self within marriage even when, for all time, marriage has always been about two people becoming one. The land of leniency toward women in reasonable divorce cases, especially in the state of New York. Oftentimes I cannot help but wonder if the world shouldn't do better at contextualizing marital vows, especially the promise of "for better, for worse."

I stated that I became accustomed to not choosing my own happiness. Let me elucidate better on that. I could have chosen to divorce my ex-wife long before she initiated it. Years before, I had been aware of our incompatibility and that it was wide enough to make me descend into unhappiness. We were friends, and I was fine with the limitations that existed within our coexistence. For several years, I kept reminding myself of how I met her and my promise to marry her just so her mean and horrific family members would not have the last laugh and learn that no matter what, every human being is valuable. I became accustomed to not prioritizing my personal happiness because it came across as selfish and cruel. I would have been battered by guilt. To me, I had to do right by staying with her. I had to keep my promises and stay true to my word. Yet for this reason, I would later become entangled in waves of depression. Had I been wrong in suppressing my own happiness? Maybe I was, maybe I wasn't. All I know is that I learned a lot from my divorce experience. I came out of it mentally stronger and wiser about life. I truly wish my ex-wife happiness. We are not in touch to date as I respected her need for privacy and separation.

Upon our divorce, a young family member who is a devout Christian told me with so much confidence that God grants no happiness in post-divorce life. I smiled a quiet smile, the type of smile that holds its peace. I chose silence so he could feel good about the ideologies he held dear. Such audacious statements define many of his kind, so it didn't come as a surprise, and I cannot say I blame him for his mindset. My humility and refusal to pry his beliefs from him allowed me to start a quiet conversation with my inner man and unleash the energy I would need to propel me to new heights.

Is marriage something I would be willing to give another trial? Currently, marriage is not on my bucket list. I feel at peace without it. I'm open-minded enough to know that a soulmate could cross my path in the future and a relationship could develop. A homeless man once told me that life is filled with surprises. In a world of uncertainty and upheaval, unshakable love stories do exist. And this belief is not just powered by what I have seen in the movies. Due to my experience and everything I have observed about marriage, I have learned not to give any advice about it.

My worldviews, though, have never changed. There is no one-size-fits-all approach. People get married weeks after a whirlwind romance and sustain it forever. Others maintain a relationship for years, but they still end up divorced. I believed, and I'll always believe, that marriage can last a lifetime if it is encased within the selfless love of both parties. Marriage should not be a benchmark for true happiness or viewed as an absolute necessity. Divorced women and men are capable of building a happier life, based on other metrics, whether or not they have love partners. The worldviews of society, other humans, or their opinions hold no power in defining our destiny unless we willingly decide to give up our inner power.

I guess it is safe to say that my profound loneliness as an immigrant, the deaths of my two best friends, coupled with my failed marriage all converged together to propel me to somewhere bigger—a redefining of coexistence between "Humans and Me."

CHAPTER **6**

The Humans and Me

Humans—the most complex, contradictory, arduous, and two-dimensional beings on earth. Ever evolving, transcendental, and transformational. Fickle and feeble. I have gone through much joy and pain in their hands, much laughter, tears, sadness, and happiness. My experiences have been so varied and life-changing that I had to have a separate chapter just to discuss them. Humans have refused to believe and understand that white, black, red, Caucasian, or brown, we're all the same. We are all one interconnected race. Humans are the direct proponents and instigators of racism.

Racism is decisively complex because humans have deemed it to be so. At its core roots, racism is accepted because it is a rigid ideology many people believe in. Yes, racism is ideological. It stems from age-old beliefs and practices, and today it is well embedded in mainstream political, economic, cultural, and basic life. At times, in America, people are killed and marginalized for the color of their skin. At times, in America, people are refused opportunities due to the color of their skin. At times, in America, people are worried even when they are walking downtown just because of the color of their skin. A long, towering structure of prejudice and discrimination that men like Dr. King, Malcolm X, and Kennedy practically gave up their lives for still relentlessly haunts the black lives. It took me some time to understand that my response to racism was what mattered the most. It took me some time to realize that I had to define myself for myself instead of letting others define me for me.

I also realized that because racism has been brandished so much in today's world, it has bred a sickening inferiority complex among too many blacks, even in their own countries. Consciously, blacks have accepted a lower place in the world that does not in any way belong to them. Worse still, they are not above plummeting themselves and their fellow blacks into the ground just to elevate a member of the white race. Perhaps out of all the side effects of racism, this is perhaps the most saddening. People like to avoid your eyes or mutter something defensively bland to get you to shut up when you try to have these honest discussions in person. As usual, since it is stories that give birth to insight, I've got a few stories to share.

I encountered racism a few times. I'll be honest. In my relationship with humans, it hasn't been all bad and racist. I'll be sharing the good too.

The first instance left an indelible memory because it happened where I did not expect it. It took place in my academic unit nine years ago. A colleague of mine, during a search committee discussion about potential candidates, bluntly told me that we had enough Africans in our department when I pointed out that one female candidate from our shortlist, a Maghrebi, had strong qualifications that matched our needs.

At the time, I was the only African out of twenty-two faculty. The remark not only astonished but also disgusted me. It hit me in the guts. I felt rejected, insulted, and discriminated against, although the comment applied to an unknown candidate. The comment targeted the candidate's African origin rather than her qualifications. As a person of color, that was not acceptable to me. It should not either have been acceptable to any of the other three colleagues who were in attendance as members of that search committee. They were white. They made no comment. I didn't either. I was a junior faculty, only in my third year, not yet grounded in my intellectual and academic journey as a university professor. Nevertheless, the racist comment did not sit well with me. It never did.

The comment "We have enough Africans in our department" haunted me days and nights for the next two months. I just couldn't let it go. I decided to act, but I had two options. I could either go after the senior faculty in question and seek some sort of "reparation," or I would leave that environment. At the time, I chose the latter. I felt like it was not necessary to go after the senior colleague because, from experience, once I start a fight, I always end it, and the fight, in this case, for it to be satisfactory to me, would need to have some repercussion on the colleague's employment. The senior colleague was an eminent scholar, and I chose not to try to ruin the colleague's years of investment in the college.

Three months after the incident, I submitted my resignation letter to my department and to the college. Once my resignation was made known in my department, the senior faculty did not show any remorse and proceeded to ask the chairman to start a search for my replacement. What happened next took me by surprise. My university's top leaders, the provost and the president, asked to meet with me. Their request to meet with me was something I did not expect. And even more so, after meeting with me individually and a third time together as a group, their persistence that I stay as a faculty at their college and not leave deeply touched me.

By the way, right after the incident with my senior colleague, when I made up my mind to leave that environment, I shared my intentions with former professors of mine from my graduate school in North Carolina, and within a month, they successfully convinced their university leaders to open a full-time position for me in their department. Their written contract came in with much higher pay than what I was getting at my campus. I shared that news with my campus provost and president and respectfully reiterated to them that I would not work in an academic unit where I could end up being judged not by my professional competence but by my national origin or skin color.

The provost and the president stunned me further with their persistence that I stay and promised that they would never condone such an unjust scenario regardless of faculty ranks. I stayed, for a lower salary than what North Carolina proposed. In the end, I stayed because my university leaders valued who I was. And over the years, I realized that I had made the right decision.

My relationship with my senior colleague improved and became productive; everyone deserves a second chance. I witnessed many positive changes take place at my institution in the decade that followed, not because of my own incident but because the leadership constantly strived to implement a culture of equity, diversity, belonging, and mutual respect. And above all, it seemed to me that I was able to stay because the most important commodity in life for me has never been monetary or financial gains but my dignity. I always give respect because I expect to get it back.

Sixteen years ago, I visited my older brother B. K. A. in Douai, a small city located in Northern France, about 120 miles from the capital city of Paris.

At that time, my brother was completing his post-doctoral medical residency in the city's main hospital, perfecting his specialty as a medical surgeon. On the day of my arrival, we left the Charles de Gaulle International Airport for the center of Paris, where we decided to spend the day before heading out to Douai the following day.

On getting to the Gare Du Nord, one of the major train stations in Paris, as I was walking down one of the large and crowded halls of the station with my brother, six heavily armed policemen suddenly surrounded us. At first it seemed surreal. We were calm and quiet, inwardly wondering what on earth was going on. One of the armed French police asked where we were heading to. My brother had the decency to respond, but I stubbornly remained silent, looking at them defiantly. The policeman then asked that we show them our documents that proved our legal status in their country. At this hour, the hall was crowded. Many people were walking by and observing the scene. Others stopped just to watch the live show, and in a split second, I realized what was going on.

We were being stopped because we were black. *Black* rhymes with *immigrant*, and *immigrant* rhymes with *potential illegal resident*, while *illegal black resident* rhymes with *subhuman* in the eyes of right-wing French politics. I whispered to my soul, "Oh no, they didn't!" I felt denigrated as a free human being.

I turned to my brother and asked loudly enough for the six policemen to hear, "Is what I am seeing truly happening?"

My brother decided to show them his identification because the crowd around us had gotten bigger. Most were white, but many black faces were staring as well, perhaps feeling worried and sorry for two fellow brothers who were about to be deported and tossed out the borders.

"What on earth is happening, B. K. A.? Just what is the meaning of this nonsense?" I asked with controlled fury, loud enough for the officers to hear.

My older brother was keeping cool under fire. "It's okay, just show them your passport, and everything will be okay."

"Show them my passport? Hell no! That's not going to happen," I told my brother firmly, without giving room for dissent.

Before my brother could respond, I turned to the officer who looked like the one in charge. "What right do you have to subject my brother and me to this? Why do you think you can stop us for no reason and treat us like subhumans?"

"Sir, I'm going to have to ask you to open your carry-on," the officer replied stiffly. Selective deafness. He had obviously chosen to ignore my question.

"Firstly, I am not opening any carry-on. Secondly, I'm not going to tolerate denigration. Thirdly, I have no reason to stand here any longer and endure your xenophobic conduct. If other people have stayed silent to tolerate this rubbish, please do not believe I will stand for it because I won't."

I could feel B. K. A.'s eyes pleading with me. He felt I was making a fuss.

"Haven't your ancestors done enough on our continent? How sure are you that some of the white people in the crowd are not illegal immigrants? They are above your foul treatment because they are whites?" I continued unperturbed as the policemen continued to stare at me. "Why not go bother someone else instead?" I said condescendingly.

I did not open my carry-on, nor did I show them any form of identification. I simply pulled out my carry-on and walked away with my brother, who seemed dumbfounded. On many of the faces of the onlookers, especially the black ones, I could see a feeling of pride.

The six policemen watched us just walk away. They, surprisingly, just let us go. It's possible that they understood from my lecturing that I was not a resident of France and, most importantly, I was not impressed by the privilege of their whiteness, nor did their attempt to embarrass us impress me. It repulsed me, and I made that fact clear.

Why would I, or anyone else, believe in any race's superiority? Why would I, or anyone else, believe in white supremacy? Why would I, or anyone else, condone racism from any race or even bow to it? These questions are sensitive but legitimate ones. There's no reason whatsoever for that to be a norm other than the psychological impact of the ugly past wreaked upon humanity by humanity. What most people fail to understand is this: Rationalization is a very powerful force. We all rationalize our ways into a series of choices, and the choices gradually define what we become.

The complex of superiority and the complex of inferiority were rationalized throughout history with regard to the human race. Sadly, many nowadays are still victims of that unfortunate societal rationalization. Here's another story to further buttress my point.

Ten years ago, I took my first group of American students to the beautiful nation of Senegal on the summer study-abroad program that I created. As a university professor in Upstate New York, it was the most rewarding experience for my students and me to have our learning experience in Senegal. A country where political stability and democratic transitions are exemplary, in addition to being a land that blends modern amenities with the cultures and traditions of diverse ethnic groups.

On my first trip with my students, we spent the first night in an apartment building before the students were placed in their host families. It was a four-floor building with a couple of apartments per floor. The reservations were taken care of by employees at our partner institution in Senegal. The apartment that was reserved for me was nice, the only one in the building with a balcony. On the first day of our arrival, we had lunch at a nearby local restaurant and then left our residence building for a guided bus tour of the city of Dakar. The tour was breathtakingly beautiful, showing us major landmarks and the main tourist attractions of the city.

Upon our return to the apartment building, I went up to my apartment and noticed my luggage packed outside in the hallway near a seating area.

I was puzzled because my luggage was inside my apartment before I left, so what had happened? I called the program partner institution, and one of their leaders in charge of all the logistics asked that I wait for him, telling me he would sort everything out as soon as he got there. In the meantime, I sat in the seating area, which was just across from the door to my reserved apartment. Just a minute later, two people came out of my apartment. Two young people—a man and a woman—apparently a very lovely young white couple. They smiled at me in greeting and went on their merry way. Nice folks, it seemed, but how did they end up in my apartment? That was the question.

A lot of thoughts crossed my mind. I decided to wait patiently for our Senegalese program partner. He arrived five minutes later, and he apologized for the inconvenience I experienced. He explained that they needed to take me to a different apartment.

"Why is that?" I asked.

He was hesitant and reluctant, as though he couldn't quite explain or did not wish to explain. I insisted, and he confessed that the younger couple also came to Dakar through their institution, and when they arrived at the same residence my group was staying at, they requested an apartment with a balcony. My apartment was the only one that had a balcony, so they made the switch. He then quickly added that the new apartment downstairs where I could go was "very nice." It was stunning, and he was sure I would love it. He confirmed that my apartment with the balcony was reserved under my name, and the change was made when my group and I were touring the city to accommodate the two white visitors.

I stared at him in disbelief. I couldn't believe it. I asked immediately to speak with the director of our partner institution. He too proceeded to join us a short moment after. We then had a serious conversation about how regrettable and how damaging their inferiority complex could be for people who look like them. Encouraging the rationalization of any race as an inferior race is not acceptable. They repeatedly apologized and repeatedly assured me that I would like my new room. They clearly missed my point. I explained my disappointment was not about the physical space I was assigned. It was about my dignity, their dignity, and our collective dignity.

I asked them to go on and apologize to the young white couple for their mishandling of the situation and ask the couple to leave my apartment because what happened should never have happened. Only then did they realize that I was not joking, and at that moment, the couple in question walked by. I greeted them and briefly explained the situation: They needed to move to a different apartment, and they moved. Justice was served. I have been looked down upon as a black person on numerous occasions in Western countries. However, because of the superiority complex prevalent on the African continent, sometimes my fellow blacks carry on a complex of inferiority when dealing with white people. I do not have such a complex, nor will I ever do. None of us, regardless of race, should ever have such a complex.

Five years ago, I went to a bar with a very good friend of mine, a male white colleague. We were seated at the bar sipping Blue Moon, the popular Belgian beer. I hardly drink. I only prefer to drink on rare occasions. I'm not a big fan of alcohol, and I've never smoked anything in my life, but when I do get the chance to drink something in a casual situation with a good friend, I usually go for something on the sweet side like a rosé, a cider, a fruity beer, or a martini.

They were playing a variety of music in the bar—hip-hop, reggae, pop, country, soul, blues, and more. I love good music regardless of the genre. Good music and inspiring lyrics are always my favorite. So here I was, enjoying the company of a great friend, a good beer, and lovely music. I noticed a black man a few feet away, at a table by himself, who glanced casually at me a couple of times. Then he summoned enough courage to walk toward my friend and me. He greeted us, and we responded back. He sounded friendly. He asked for my name, and after I responded, he asked me where I was from. I responded politely. Usually, after people ask about my origin, they proceed to ask me questions about my country, culture, and so on, or they move to a different topic entirely.

He did the latter, but he took me by surprise when he boldly stated, "You and your people sold my ancestors."

It wasn't just the abrupt shock of the words or the way the mood of the conversation shifted. It was his tone riddled with accusation and the burning conviction in his eyes.

I looked at my white colleague, who stared helplessly at me, and we both looked back at the black man, unable to string coherent words together. The man had knocked the wind out of us.

I took a deep breath and responded, "Brother, I don't remember selling anyone. However, if what you are referring to is the transatlantic slave trade, then it's a discussion worth having in a historical context. Why not have a seat? What did you say your name was, and where are you from?"

The stranger did not know which part of Africa his ancestors came from. He said so. That was part of his argument that because of slavery and Africans selling Africans to Europeans, some of them no longer have a nation or a place in Africa to call home. I connected with his pain about feeling "nationless."

In reality, home is a complex construct. How do we, or should we, define home? Where do we belong, or should we claim to belong? Unfortunately, because of slavery, some African Americans look down on Africans, as they buy into the ignorance nurtured in America by stereotypes about Africa and Africans. Similarly, some Africans fear African Americans, as they buy into the culture of black violence in America portrayed in Western media to unfairly criminalize the whole community of African Americans.

It is up to black people worldwide to transcend their undeniable malaise toward each other, a malaise successfully planted in our souls mainly by the former colonizers through their divide-and-conquer tactics, but also from our own mistakes and our inability to overcome the superficial that kept us divided. It is up to black people to be united, to plot the positive trajectory of their race, our race, and to rid ourselves of the stereotypes whites projected on blacks from centuries of domination and exploitation. Equally importantly, the stereotypes blacks sadly project on each other.

The conversation was shaky and awkward at first. As I shared historical facts with him, he became more relaxed and open-minded. Yes, it was true that Africans were involved in catching their own for the European slave trader. Yet these same Africans were also subjected to a horrible reality. They were given weapons by the Europeans to capture other Africans from other tribes, or else the weapons would go to the other tribes to capture them, in which they themselves would become enslaved. It was as though the Europeans successfully pitted us against each other, turning the avoidance of the slave trade into a battle of survival. That wasn't all. Many other factors were also involved. It was a story riddled with a lot of tapestries and mysteries.

As we continued the conversation, it slowly started to turn civil. My work colleague was at times uncomfortable with the particular line of conversation, and he gracefully left it to me.

What happened in that bar with that fellow African American was not the only time I experienced such an encounter. Race relations have their complexity even within the same race and the same skin color. Pan-Africanist movements have historically worked hard to unite black people from all over the world, especially those from the United States in Africa. Men like Marcus Garvey and W. E. B. Dubois dedicated their whole lives to this. Nevertheless, the divide-and-conquer methods used by Europe and slave traders from the fifteenth to the nineteenth centuries still continue to have some societal sequelae within the modern global black community. I do believe, though, that one day all black people around the world will thrive in the true spirit of Pan-Africanism.

All my aforementioned stories have two things in common: race and identity. A long time ago, I learned that these two are conjoined by intricate threads. If I was going to survive as a black man in the Western world, I needed to understand certain things that would influence and project my confidence to the outside world.

The first thing I understood was the discovery of and connection with my inside voice. That led me to the understanding that one has the power to not become what they are defined as by other people or a given society. In most declarations of independence or constitutions around the world, citizens are defined to be created equal. The American Declaration, for instance, reads:

> We hold these truths to be self-evident, that all men are created equal, that they are endowed by their Creator with certain unalienable Rights, among these are Life, Liberty and the pursuit of Happiness.

Clearly, when Africans were brought to America as enslaved people and treated as subhumans, enslavers did not hold true to the text in their Declaration of Independence. They were, therefore, villains in many regards. In Europe, as well, they viewed black people as subhumans when they started the inhumane slave trade commerce in the fifteenth century. In some European regions today, some Europeans, both the educated and the uneducated, continue to cast disgust about the presence of immigrants from African nations.

Those are facts we must live with, yet they are phenomena that have no business being alive in this age when the world is becoming more and more interconnected and more creolized. To me, even if I am regarded by another human being as an inferior being because of my race or origin, only I have the power to feel inferior and thus become inferior. My inside voice forbids such self-denigration. As a black man in the Western world, my self-confidence remains strong regardless of the inequality and social injustice faced by minorities. There is no doubt in my mind that I am a child of the universe no less than the trees and the stars, and I, too, have a right to be here.

I said at the beginning of this chapter that I have been fortunate enough to also have wonderful and inspiring racial experiences. Racial experiences have had many positive outcomes between humans and me, especially with regard to my American students. Being a university professor has been the most fulfilling joy of my adult life. It comes with a vastitude of opportunities for intellectual growth, learning, discoveries, and inspiring experiences.

From travels to campuses across the United States and abroad for research or conference presentations, to the creation of innovative, thought-provoking courses, my journey in the field has been humbling. In the past twelve years, I have taught a very diverse racial group of students, yet predominantly white. The topics that I teach are meant to deconstruct biased caricatures about Africa while also giving my students the tools to distinguish between single stories and balanced stories. Both my students of color and my white students appreciate the critical-thinking skills embedded in my course learning outcomes.

Usually, my students quickly overlook what makes me different from them, my Africanity, and genuinely value what connects me to them, my human race. As the years go by and my seniority starts shaping firm and tangible, another feeling of elevation has been taking form: Seeing what my students from my junior years in teaching have become in their professional lives. They are breaking boundaries and shattering glass ceilings. What an amazing feeling!

Some of them are already PhD holders. Others recently became my colleagues in the same field. Some are medical doctors, dentists, pharmacists, nurses, paramedics, and a few others are lawyers, district attorneys, public defenders, business owners, banking officers, government agency professionals, freelance and creative writers, and even politicians. I have also heard from a handful who became special education or K-12 schoolteachers or administrators, nongovernmental organization leaders, engineers, data or policy analysts, archaeologists, librarians, and office managers. Many more are out there doing their best. It is fair to confess that most of these amazing students who once took one or more of my classes also inspired me in many ways with their great minds.

As much as I am tempted to name them all to show my gratitude for the fulfillment they added to my life as a black university faculty, the list would have been too long for such a tiny chapter of my memoir. Two names, however, are exceptionally worth squeezing in here. The first, C. P.-M., is a black Haitian American, and the second, H. N. K., is a white American. Their exceptionalism, together with all the great minds I now call former students of mine, pushed me to do better, hence helping me become a better critical thinker and servant of the profession.

Former student C. P.-M. was a top-ranked student in my classes and graduated two years after I began my university professor career. C. P.-M. went on to teach in charter schools and other community-based schools and served a year with the educational group City Year, followed by two years in Peace Corps. Then she began a glittering career within a US government agency while also completing graduate studies. She graduated at the top of her graduate program. I could not be prouder and more honored to nowadays call C. P.-M. a good friend and an inspiration for the generation currently in college.

Former student H. N. K. graduated only six years ago, but the list of achievements she has scored ever since is impressive. H. N. K. was a brilliant mind in my classes, studied abroad for a semester, and decided to move to Africa upon graduation. Quite unusual, but six years later, H. N. K. is still in Africa. After an English teacher position for two years, H. N. K. worked for a UN Sustainable Development Group as a fellow, then for a Global Research and Advocacy Group focused on female reproductive health. She was successively hired for better positions with UNESCO, the Clinton Health Access Initiative, and the Bill & Melinda Gates Institute for Population and Reproductive Health. All these positions held by H. N. K.

were based in Africa. At times her position put her in charge of a portfolio consisting of many countries throughout the francophone West and Central African region. I feel blessed to witness stories such as those of C. P.-M. and H, N. K., and of many other alumni, unfold before my eyes. They, my former and current students, are some of the most amazing humans in my life.

My life story and the story of some of my students have taught me that irrespective of skin color, time, distance, or limitations, Africans can rise, soar, achieve, and become groundbreaking in all spheres if they set their minds to it. We do not have to be stifled by our past or even our present experiences. We can be a strong, pervasive force if we choose.

And for my African-American brothers and sisters who still feel lost and resentful because they are not sure where their story fits in the story of the world or because their heritage, ancestry, and origin still feel steeped and chained in complexities stemming from slavery, imperialism, and capitalism, here is a poem for you. I wrote this poem a few days after my encounter with my African-American brother at the bar. It's just one in my large collection of poems that I write each time a life event happens and causes me to immortalize the moment in poetic verses. I have decided to release it within the pages of this memoir. I named it "Rearview Mirror," and I hope it resonates with you.

> *You sold my very great-grandparents*
> *To the white enslavers, my brother.*
>
> *Oh really, please enlighten me on my guilt*
> *because memories have escaped my home.*

I warn you, foreign brother, from mockery
Because my wounds still hurt from the past.

Let's then have a frank conversation, my dear
About whom to blame from a world long gone.

Are you saying your people are innocent
For what happened in Goree and Elmina?

My people, unlike politicians or Europeans
They are disgusted with errors from their past.

Then how would you repair the despair in me?
As I try to live in peace with a brother in pieces?

Am I to be blamed for what I vomited, undefeated
Which, still, is a fact in history, a fact not to repeat?

My brother, forgive my rage; I now comprehend
You're sorry just as I should; we're born in their sin.

I am the new African, the neo-African American.
Freed from naivety and slavery upon Humanity.

So, brother, my dear brother, what to do now?

While I fix the rearview mirror, what about a hug?

CHAPTER 7

Realms of My Spirituality: Accepting of Self and Other

What is religion?

A sociocultural structure of prescribed manners and methods, worldviews, sanctified places, passages, revelations, principles, or organizations that are interrelated with supernatural, transcendental, and spiritual elements. It's the belief in vast but unseen supremacy that holds the world in a gentle clasp. A well-oiled organization and system that governs people's lives in distinctive forms.

My fundamental and simplistic definition is that it is a particular system of faith and worship of God or the supernatural. Ultimately, members of a religion, through their faith, grow strong spiritually. In essence, religions, for many, improve health, learning, economic well-being, self-control, self-esteem, and empathy. Many believers do get blessed in life through their faith. Others aren't so lucky.

I know that race and religion are both touchy and sensitive topics. I have already touched on the topic of race in the previous chapter, and now I will be doing the same for religion here in this chapter.

I have nothing against religion. In fact, I was born and bred Catholic. I was raised Catholic, baptized Catholic, and sent to a Catholic elementary school. Religion was thoroughly embedded in my life at a young age without my permission. There was no real or true fervency in my Catholicism. I was just as Catholic as any Catholic child. My family and friends attended the Catholic Church as well while growing up. We all met religious practices in this world, and we all simply toed the line and followed directions. It never occurred to anyone to question concepts or context. It never occurred to us to espouse it, even though we might have never fully understood it. Although my religious reforms have gone through vast transformations, I do not in any way resent or belittle those who hold on steadfastly to religion. It is a choice.

I have absolutely no quarrels with believers. It's admirable to believe in something and to have faith in something. Humans are spirit beings, and many of us are connected to our spirits and souls more than others. Everything spiritual practitioners believe in is all well and good. However, a long time ago, I became quite convinced that religious life does not and will never work for me. You see, there are aspects of religion that I do not trust.

For one, I don't trust religions that indirectly endorse violence. You find right-wing politicians and Christian priests praising the glory of the Christian faith, yet couldn't this be more ironic? After all, you also find Christian priests praying for those who go to war to kill other human beings. You have to ask yourself, are these human beings not fathers, sons, and brothers? Why would priests pray fervently for the victory of their countrymen going to war? Why do religious leaders and influencers pray for their people to slaughter their enemies? How is war justifiable? Why do members of the Christian faith feel it's okay to simply tailor religion according to their preferences?

I was taught that in the sixth commandment, God has clearly stated that we should not kill, which means that God wants us to protect human life. Protect, not eliminate. Perhaps killing an enemy is an acceptable killing. Should we call this hypocrisy or rationality? One may argue that killing during a war is a necessity. The church had enormous influence over the people of Medieval Europe and had the power to make laws and influence great monarchs. When I read about the "great" history from back then, I struggled to reconcile my Christian faith and the Bible. Slavery also happened with the complicity of the church. It lasted for four centuries. Some church founders, churchgoers, and even the churches themselves had enslaved people, yet the Holy Bible asked us to treat others the way we would like to be treated. Now, should we also call this hypocrisy, or is there any rationality here?

During the era of colonization, especially after the Berlin Conference in the late nineteenth century where African lands were divided among European nations at the expense of the African people, many of these African regions were severely abused economically and their people physically. In the Congo region, for instance, in the mission letter that King Leopold II of Belgium assigned to his religious colonial Missionaries, he wrote:

You will certainly go to evangelize, but your evangelization must inspire, above all, Belgium's interests. Your principal objective in our mission in the congo is never to teach the niggers to know God. This they know already. They speak and submit to a Mungu, one Nzambi, one Nzakomba, and what else I don't know. They know that killing or sleeping with someone else's wife is bad. Have the courage to admit it; you are not going to teach them what they already know. Your essential role is to facilitate the task of administrators and industrialists, which means you will go to interpret the gospel in the way it will be the best to protect your interests in that part of the world.

The missionaries did just that. Some of them even had no issues with going overboard. Let's not forget what Belgium did to African heroes like Patrice Lumumba in order to "protect their interests." But I digress. Is it hypocritical or rational to claim to be a Christian and not follow the ninth commandment of the Bible? The ninth commandment states that we should not bear false witness, which means do not tell a lie. Do not tell stories that are untrue about people.

The modern era, starting with the second half of the twentieth century, still witnesses some churchgoers kill each other, steal, distort, lie, manipulate, and commit all kinds of unspeakable atrocious activities. Most people spread the cloak of religion over their petty desires, while others use religious beliefs and practices to justify and perpetuate a lot of inhumane activities.

"What about the political leaders that suddenly have religious affiliations when they want to contest for office?" I asked an overzealous Christian friend after he voted for a crooked politician.

"What about some celebrities with shitty morals who randomly give praise to God for their success when they appear in public spaces?" I asked another overzealous Christian friend who was an avid fan of Hollywood.

They shrugged indifferently. "What about them?"

"Wouldn't you say that they are questionable and they reflect badly on everything religions claim to morally uphold?"

I might sound judgmental, but the art of writing is, in essence, judgmental. You're either judging yourself or judging the society around you, but there is always some form of judgment emanating from true reflection. There are many wrongs and deep-seated, complex ideologies that characterize the world of religion.

I dropped the Catholic faith because, like many other religious faiths, Catholics claim things they cannot prove. In short, most of the texts in the Bible cannot be proven, although some believers claim the opposite to no concrete avail. However, I know that I exist because I am. And I decided to believe in my singular existence and strengthen the spiritual voice in me rather than abiding by the teaching of any organized religious group of faith based on a holy book that cannot be proven to me as factual. Ever since I found myself on my own spiritual journey, I have had a more meaningful life. One cannot and should not change a winning team.

Many of the ten commandments in the Bible are barely respected by Christians, even by their leaders. The simple fact that a Catholic priest or bishop or any other religious leader would give benediction to their countrymen going to war, among other political behaviors, is hypocritical. The fact that churchgoers commit sins on a daily basis—when they get mad at someone, lose their temper, curse at someone, or entertain violence or disrespect—is hypocritical. Others go as far as casting someone out on the basis of different political or religious views; avoiding friendship because of skin color, sexual orientation, or national origin; and envying or lying, or being greedy for financial gain. Equally disturbing are those who claim or think to know better than the people not from their faith group; they actually contradict the biblical portrait of a Christian or a religious person.

With my inside voice, I cannot cheat because I remain myself. With my inside voice, life is about a simple principle: action, consequence, and responsibility. I, therefore, take full responsibility for my actions when I am wrong. I do not get to confide in any divinity to have my sins forgiven. I learn from my mistakes and try to do better moving forward. All human brains are wired for morality: self-awareness of right and wrong is, therefore, universally innate. The human ability to act upon their most basic urges and desires, whether wrong or right, depends on the strength of the inside voice or—as the religious name it—the strength of their faith. As detailed in my spiritual connection with life and death, as well as my journey as a living being among my peers called humans, faith is a process that I understand as an important step to unleashing energies that make things happen. I get that result on my own, and I am at peace.

Throughout the course of my college education, my graduation, and my departure from Togo to the United States, I started to ask a lot of questions about Christianity, to which I could not get a satisfying response. For most of the questions I asked, all I got was a response based on faith. I understood what faith entailed back then, and I still do now. I just needed more than that. I did not want to question the validity of my Catholic teachings. I only wanted to connect the dots that would be rationalized in my ever-evolving mind about existence, so I spoke to many Christians and priests about it, and some got irritated with my endless follow-up questions.

A lot of my Christian friends thought that I was lost and naive and I would find my way back to Christ with prayers. They never understood I had no quarrels with them, nor did they understand that I never felt better than them. They did not understand me as much as I really needed them to. I studied the Bible, yet it could give no real answers. I soon discovered that many do not follow the Bible, but they would clutch it tighter than a pillow or quote from it better than literature professors discussing their favorite novels. I was told several times not to base my faith on people's inconsistencies but rather on my faith in God. Great. Except that I had complex and burning questions I couldn't rid myself of.

A few people in my family were Jehovah's Witnesses. They sparked my inner curiosity, and I allowed myself to listen to them and their preaching every time they jumped on an opportunity to make me understand that they were the one true Christian church capable of leading me to the Almighty Jehovah. I appreciated their confidence, but then I couldn't resist asking my usual questions—the questions that call for straight answers beyond the realms of faith. Everything I got was downright evasive, deviating from the main point and giving me answers revolving around faith, trust, and belief. Yet through these half-baked concepts, these folks wanted me to have a total paradigm shift. The question was, how? How on earth was that supposed to happen?

Many of them could not even reflect on the questions because they felt blasphemous. The intellectualization of the gospel was viewed predominantly as sacrilegious. I know I have been taught not to question my faith, but the more I grow older, the more I start to understand my own existence, and the more I understand that it is okay to be different and to disagree without being disagreeable. It is vital for me to exist through the lens of my spirituality while seeing the value in the existence of others and their own beliefs. As I began slowly but surely my road to Renaissance, I gained meaningful fulfillment that I had never experienced before in my life. My inner voice opened up my senses to what appears to me as the three dimensions of our spiritual world. The physical dimension, the metaphysical dimension, and the afterlife.

The physical dimension of the spiritual world is limited to the observable and is thus restricted to what we have in our universe. That includes most religious faith believers who pray to God and leave everything in the hand of God to decide about their life. In sum, God is in control of their life, their joys and sorrows, their destiny. They are human servants of the divine Almighty. They are, therefore, not divine themselves, though they believe to have been created in the image of God.

The metaphysical dimension of the spiritual world is unseeable to the eyes of regular mortals. The few humans who learned to cross into that dimension develop the ability to see elements of nature that await to serve them from the invisible world. In Christianity, they are portrayed as angels. The only problem is that most Christians think about the afterlife when they think of angels. That is because they are not taught, at their level as servants of God, to become divine themselves.

But the few humans that develop their spirituality beyond the confinement of organized faith groups are able to cross into the nonmythical space of elements of nature, namely angels. These serviceable elements abound in water, fire, air, and land in the form of energies. To cross over to them is to connect to the energies that define them. And since our inside voice is energy, one must first learn to communicate with their inside voice to be introduced to the elements of the invisible world.

Of course, some religious leaders, not all of them, find their way to the metaphysical dimension when they reach the energetic spiritual height they do not disclose to their followers. Some traditional practitioners, not all of them, also get there when they properly evoke the right combination of energies still lingering in our natural environment.

The afterlife is the world of energies after the human body becomes lifeless, that is, after death. The idea of hell and heaven after life is nice. But are people who terribly suffer in this world and die in lamentable conditions really going to a "heaven" with white angels somewhere beyond the skies if they live an exemplary, religious life in their misery, as taught by some organized religions? The answer to heaven after death is not tangible but certainly tentative. For such an unfortunate human who lived in misery, I see a life on earth that was already hell. There are also humans who live a life of heaven on earth, filled with joy and tremendous blessings.

The inside voice to cultivate is energy, and when properly nurtured, it finds its place in the metaphysical dimension after death. Many humans, at one point or another in their life, experience a feeling of déjà vu but choose to ignore what it might mean. All that I would disclose here is that for the humans who become the few, the déjà vu feeling loses its mythical connotation. These days, I feel complete. I am aware that I am misunderstood by many, but I am not alone. My followers may be invisible, but my peers are understanding.

Today I am no longer a member of any religion, but I am the owner of my spirituality. I do not claim that religions are not spiritual; they are, but they are organized forms of spirituality that operate through a set of organized practices. I left the organized dimension of my spirituality and became more of an individual practitioner. One that has to do with having a sense of peace and purpose. Unapologetically, I own my successes and failures, my joys and sorrows, my open-mindedness and unintended biases. I also fully believe in my commitment to be free at heart, to believe in the little things in my life and not in superficial things. I believe in getting up each time I fall, learning from my mistakes, and believing in the hero in me.

Some call it the power of positive thinking.

I simply say, I am my own temple.

The profound loneliness I experienced in my early years in the United States turned out to be the most pivotal and most important moments that allowed me to discover myself and connect the unanswered dots within my inner self. The ability to think about the unusual, question the ordinary, and reflect on my own existence opened doors to the very little things in life that escaped my attention while growing up. Questions such as the following:

Why do we fear the things that frighten us?
Why do we crave love for other human beings?

Why do we feel hurt when death robs us of a beloved person?

Why can we not have a conversation with the furniture around us? With the birds outside our walls? With animals in their natural domesticated environment? With trees in the garden and the souls of the dead? Is it rational or impossible?

Why are we vulnerable?

In sum, why do we exist?

There are many responses from serious or critical minds out there who have given most of the answers. Most of the answers I knew to those unusual interrogations were derived from social constructs that witnessed my growth as an inhabitant of planet Earth. Loneliness permitted me a much-needed escape from our amazing but noisy world and enabled the discovery of the power of the internal voice trapped inside the living being called me.

For clarification, true believers of religious faith, at times, have ascendance to what could be called a divine call. The power of faith can unleash internal energies that I do not deny. Yet it has been evident in my life that humans can reach on their own, stand, appreciate, and become the sole commander of the internal power in them without going through a third party, namely God. Therefore my relationship with God is not reflective of any denial or repudiation of a higher power, but it only reflects my spiritual autonomy.

Again, I am my own temple.

Most humans are afraid of the afterlife. For many of them, religions guarantee their journey beyond their life on Earth.

Apart from the fact that no human being has yet returned from the dead to give us a lively and colorful description of heaven or hell, my temple allows me to leave peacefully, uncontained, unconditioned, unrestricted, yet consciously aware of right and wrong, keenly invested in treating humans as fairly as possible, regardless of whether they are Christians, Muslims, Buddhists, Hindus, Rastafarians, traditionalists, agnostics, atheists, or simply a member of any other belief system. All humans are intrinsically exposed to good and bad within their society's temptation. Temptation is, therefore, not inexistent in any community of believers. However, a strong and unshakable mindset, plus a commitment to always do better or even to get into good trouble for the right cause—the cause of justice, liberty, and freedom—is a faith from universalism that requires no denomination.

In my assessment, one can be a good friend or even be a life partner with a member of any group of faith as long as positive energies are the essence that sustains their communion. Many groups of faith do not permit crossing the line into "rival" groups. Why does there even have to be rivalry within the religion? I'll never truly understand it. This is saddening because these humans imply that their God is not the Almighty of all humans.

Isolated within my loneliness, my internal voice grew very distinct and very inclusive. It is a voice that is tolerant of religious differences. It is a voice that is tolerant of all skin colors. It is a voice that is tolerant of all national origins. It is a voice that is tolerant of all physical appearances. It is a voice that is tolerant of people with disability. It is a voice that is tolerant of different sexual orientations and genders. It is a voice that is tolerant of otherness. Martin Luther King rightfully advocated that we only judge a person by the content of the person's character. Here on planet Earth, whereas many turn to prayers to strengthen themselves mentally and emotionally during difficult times, others turn to their minds and inner energies.

Within my sole temple, when faced with hardship, the conversation is always unconventional:

Internal Voice:	What are you doing? Stand up, get off your behind, and get going.
Me:	I can't. I need help because I don't have the energy to keep going.
Internal Voice:	Take a good look in the mirror, and tell me who you really are.
Me:	I see nothing. I can't get up, and I can't get going.
Internal Voice:	I see a warrior—a winner, not a whiner. You promised never to let us down.
Me:	My apologies. You're right. Enough of my whining. I'm getting up.
Internal Voice:	Yeah! That's the spirit! Never be afraid of falling. Only be afraid of not getting back up after you fall. That is the true test of a man's character. You must never remain defeated. You must not.
Me:	I must not. I am a winner, not a whiner. I am a warrior.

This is a promise that my internal voice and I have kept alive. It is a promise that has transformed my life and the lives of those on the same path as me. It is a promise that does not fail because we always get back up. It is a promise that is conducive to building and sustaining a strong mindset amid the vicissitudes of life. This is resilience at its peak.

I would personally define *resilience* as "the ability to maintain the true self in the face of adversity and to successfully forge one's mental strength for survival." I have never asked for nor accepted a free ride in life, and I trust that my successes shall come from merit, not from favoritism. On that basis, one shall not pay for a ride that is only free to people from a specific race. A woman, for instance, shall not pay for a ride that is free to men alone, or men also shall not pay for a ride that is free to women alone. Resilience is best served when embedded in consistency. Inconsistency, I believe, opens doors to both intended and unintended acts of discrimination and unfairness. Life has never been easy or fair, and it never will be. We all mold it according to the cards we are dealt. We create and fine-tune our existence with our hands and our minds. But what goes on in mind is definitely more important. It shapes what we use our hands to become.

"You cannot wait until life isn't hard anymore before you decide to be happy," said a brave young lady diagnosed with a 2 percent cancer survival rate during *America's Got Talent* television show last year before she performed her beautiful and heartfelt original song called "It's OK." According to her, you can be happy and be going through something very hard at the same time. "You don't have to pick one or the other," she added. She was right. I found out about her only a week ago. Her strong mindset and resilience resonated with something deeply rooted in me: the untamable. I also learned that she died from her cancer six months after her performance at *America's Got Talent*. The bridge that represented her life was clearly short. Relatively short. Only thirty-one years old, she was. Nightbirde was her stage name. The day I will lose my own hide-and-seek game with death, I, too, will die, and it's okay. After all, the afterlife can't be that bad for the few who happily live and rejoice in the sound of energies. Unless Christians end up being right about their heaven and hell, in which case, well, I will still sing "It's OK" in a perfect spiritual tune.

Like many, for various reasons, I am misunderstood at times in my relationships with human beings, and it is okay not to be on the same page as others. Nevertheless, most humans and I value and appreciate positive energies. I love peace. I love tolerance, discipline, and above all, mutual respect. I give respect because I expect to get it back. My worldviews are simply human because I belong to the human race. Many might wonder that since I have harnessed the internal voice deep within and elevated my belief in human faith, does this mean I do not believe in God? This is a blunt question as to whether I'm an atheist or an agnostic. So for clarification's sake, let me answer here:

I believe in a higher spiritual power that, in my view, humans call God. I do not call it God, but calling it God wouldn't bother me either. I don't conceive of a higher spiritual power to fit the description in the Bible: a God that is watching every human's move, waiting to judge and decide humans' fate about hell or heaven when they die. I already see people living in hell on Earth; I also see people living in heaven on Earth.

I believe in a higher spiritual power because I feel it in me, I communicate with it, and I get the results I deserve on Earth.

In a simplistic way, I call it my inside voice. Hence, I need no external or organized belief system beyond my own temple. I require no religion to know right from wrong, seek internal betterment, and value other humans in their diversity. One very famous female African-American television icon, a Christian, once said during her live television show that she firmly believed that there could not be only one way to get to God, and she added that she would take full responsibility for her going to hell or heaven for believing what she believed. Many pastors and churchgoers were outraged. I agreed with her.

I am, therefore, in total harmony and peace around people from any spiritual belief as long as they accept my right to exist and they do not see other believers from outside their faith group as not good enough when these other believers also pursue positivism. Truth be told, what tangible evidence does any religious group member have that I am the one to be saved besides faith in their belief? Some of my peers, or invisible followers, call it dogmatism. I give it no name; I give it no attention.

I was there once, and now I am here. So let's all live together in peace. Let's all treat each other with love. Let's all coexist. Let's all embrace our belonging to the one and only race that matters: the human race.

Epilogue

November 2022

It's a beautiful day, but in the air hangs the threat of the end of the opulence I have come to love. As I stroll through the campus grounds, I almost mourn the end of summer. It's usually my favorite time of the year. This particular summer was peculiar and unusual. I spent every day of this summer in my study gathering the words to describe my story. Now it's done. As I come down to the end of this book, it's almost a bit surreal to believe that I'm now at the end of sharing all the pieces of my story. It has been a joyous ride, and I'm glad you have stayed with me all through it. Now that you have read up until the final chapter, I believe you are not yet fagged out from the display of my unconventional beliefs. Humans are a product of their experiences. Our lives consist of stories fashioned from these experiences, and they go on to spring forth ideological beliefs and convictions.

I expect many to be flabbergasted by my views. I expect surprise, criticism, and even subtle acceptance. I expect questions too. It is inherent within human nature for people to inevitably question the unconventional, and that's fine.

There's more I believe most people should take from my story. I do not believe I have ever considered myself a natural-

129

born winner. There are people who have everything handed to them on a platter. They don't need to plunge themselves into the depths of hard work to become brilliant successes. And then there are those who have to work hard for what they need. Golden platters do not exist for them. They move and crawl and storm their way through the valley of hard work to get to the lustrous peak of success. I admire the former, knowing I am a member of the latter. My modest achievements have been through the work of my hands and the resilience that powers my blood.

I have weathered storms and crisscrossed oceans, time, and distance to build my dreams. I dealt with the brutality of loneliness, the unprecedented power of death, and the rigorous demands of life in a foreign land to become who I am. Has it all been worth it? Yes.

Optimism has been one of the biggest driving forces in my life. It was what I felt the day I watched the slim Asian karate man beat up his adversaries. Optimism was what got me through my first freshman year when uncertainty was the thematic influence of that year. It powered my decision to leave the borders of Togo and dare to achieve more for myself. Optimism was what brought a beautiful and talented cancer patient to bless the world with her amazing voice, even in the face of her 2 percent cancer survival rate. There was so much beauty in that. It overwhelmed me so much that I couldn't speak, and it revitalized and reinvigorated my beliefs. Optimism builds resilience. Both of them are like two peas in a pod, and resilience has defined my life over and over through the best of times and through the worst of times.

Despite my modest achievements, my uncommon worldviews, and my experiences, I am still a work in progress. At forty-eight,

I am still unfolding, exploring, becoming, and unveiling. There is still more to come. There is still more I hope to achieve. The stronger inner man within me has gotten me to levels of strength and courage I never dreamed possible. And I believe it will always do the same. I have learned distinctive ways to beat adversity, transcend beyond pain and grief, and keep myself standing strong in spite of life's harsh pressures. I do hope you will learn to do the same. I hope you will realize that no one needs to come to save you before you save yourself. A hero lies in us all.

At my deepest core, I am still African. My resilience was born out of my life experience, especially after I left my home country. I am thus not against a definite return, one day, to my native country of Togo to serve in whatever capacity they or I would deem fit. And if I do decide to return, it would not be because I have something superior in my brain to share. In fact, I have nothing superior. My fellow countrymen in Togo are equal human beings equipped with equal ability to contribute greatly to our shared homeland.

Some fellows from the African diaspora consider themselves better than those who never left the motherland. It is an arrogance that defies contextualization and relativism. Equally important, if I do return to my native land, it wouldn't be as a human with less consideration for his Africanity.

Some fellow African brothers and sisters in the motherland, on the other hand, consider those of us in the diaspora as less African; that, too, is an arrogance not worthy of consideration, except in the case of Africans who migrate to the Western countries and turn their back on their African identity. Those Africans in the diaspora who turn their back on their African identity are those I shall call the "lost souls."

Understanding, assimilating, and successfully navigating Western social constructs for any African in the Western diaspora is certainly valuable and an absolute necessity. Nevertheless, in order to escape the trap of becoming an unconscious victim of the complex of mental inferiority, I urge my fellow diasporic Africans to dig deeper when they give their abroad-born children names of the neocolonizer that even they, the parents, could sometimes hardly pronounce accurately.

Let's wonder for a second about why it is that it is Africans who always delight in taking white people's names. Let's wonder for a second about why our white friends, even the most decent and humane ones who genuinely consider and treat black people as equal fellows, never give African names to their children. I have yet to come across a white person with a first name like Adebayo, Abayomi, Seynabou, Moussa, Kwami, Chiamaka, Lakeisha, Shanika, or Kodjo—not even Barack.

My point is not that white people should give African names to their children. Why should they? I suspect that they do not because they accept and embrace their Western identity, and rightfully so. Why then do so many Africans blindly delight themselves in dwelling in a constant colonized mindset? Perhaps the power dynamic between the West and Africa created a sense of betterment in taking a Western name. Yet nowadays, although all experts in geopolitics recognize that China is economically more powerful than every single country in Europe, Europeans have not been giving their children Chinese names!

Deculturalization is an unfortunate loss that no degree of assimilation into a foreign culture could make whole in terms of one's inner identity and self-belonging. My parents gave me the middle name Raymond at birth; it is French. I only went by

Epilogue

Raymond when I lived in Togo, although it was not on my birth
certificate. Luckily, I also had a first name, Kodjo; it is African.
In America, I only went by Kodjo.

If there is one thing I hope my fellow African diaspora
brothers and sisters take from this memoir, it is the awakening or
strengthening of a paradigm shift. An African name does not in any
form or shape devalue the content of one's character or intellect.
Our residence in a foreign land should not change who we are.
Our roots must, therefore, not be lost because if they are, then all
is lost. Not just for ourselves but for the incoming generation and
the younger ones who currently look up to us. Our foundational
heritage, ancestry, and beliefs in our continent must never be
subjected to change. At heart, I am deeply proud of my unshakable
dual existentialism as both an African and an American.

I will close with a quote by Kenyan renowned author Ngugi
Wa Thiong'O, with whom I was honored to conversate on a
few occasions:

> If you know all the languages of the world but not your
> mother tongue, that is enslavement. Knowing your mother
> tongue and all other languages too is empowerment.

My memoir has touched upon some really sensitive and
core issues that characterize our world. My views are largely
subjective, and no form of imposition was strategized during
the course of my writing. Storytelling has several dimensions,
many of which I correctly hope I have infused. My life is still
unfolding, and I hope that soon I will be back with another
thought-provoking book for the world to read. Until then,
I hope this serves as a suitable companion.

Printed in Great Britain
by Amazon

43585935R00088